Law Firm and Attorney Marketing: A 21st Century Guide
Marketing for Lawyers 101

This book serves as a guide to demystify law firm and attorney marketing for lawyers and law firm managers in a now global, competitive market.

Kingsley Ugochukwu Ani

Law Firm and Attorney Marketing: A 21st Century Guide

KINGSLEY UGOCHUKWU ANI.

Copyright © Kingsley Ugochukwu Ani, Esq.

All rights reserved. No part of this book may be reproduced or utilized in any form or by any means, electronic or mechanical, including photocopying, recording or by any information storage and retrieval system, without permission in writing from the author.

Amazon Paperback Edition: **ISBN** 978-1-7095-7918-9

First Edition
1 2 3 4 5 6 7 8 9 10

Limit of Liability/Disclaimer of Warranty: While the publisher and author have used their best efforts in preparing this book, they make no representations or warranties with respect to the accuracy or completeness of the contents of this book and disclaim any implied warranties of merchantability or fitness for a particular purpose. No warranty may be created or extended by sales representatives or written sales materials. The advice and strategies contained herein may not be suitable for your situation. Neither the publisher nor author shall be liable for any loss of profit or any other commercial damages, including but not limited to special, incidental, consequential, or other damages that may accrue to you for relying on the contents herein contained. Please note that this book is for information purposes.

This book is dedicated to all the lawyers in the 21st century who are willing to break away from the restrictions placed on us as Attorneys.

Remember, you have to be visible to your target audience in order to get them to buy from you.

This page is intentionally left blank.

Preface _____ *xi*

Chapter One _____ *15*

   Professional Service Firms: The Legal Services Industry in Focus _____ **15**
      Industry Torn Apart? _____ 18

Chapter Two _____ *23*

   Building a Digital Presence: The Importance of Having Online Portfolios _____ **23**

   INTRODUCTION _____ **23**

   Website Design for your Legal Practice _____ **26**
      Basics to Note: _____ 26

   Law Firm Website Preparation _____ **28**
      Law Firm Website Pages Planning _____ 29
      Crafting Content for your Law Firm Website Pages ____ 30
      Law Firm Website Design Evaluation _____ 31

   Integral Points to Note About Your Law Firm Website Design _____ **31**
      Navigation: _____ 31
      Click-To-Call _____ 32
      Call-to-Action/Lead Generation Forms _____ 32
      Use Compelling Headlines for Your Practice Areas ____ 34

   Content _____ **35**

   Case Studies _____ **37**

   Technical Points to Note for Your Law Firm website ___ **38**
      Website Speed _____ 38
      SSL Certificates _____ 39

   Taking Action for your Law Firm Website _____ **39**

Chapter Three _____ *41*

   Law Firm Content Marketing: A New Marketing Guide _ **41**
      INTRODUCTION _____ 41

   What is Content Marketing? _____ **44**

Examples of Popular Law Blogs — 45

Developing a Law Firm Content Marketing Strategy — 46
What Do Clients Want? — 47

Benefits of having a Law Firm Content Marketing Strategy — 49

Getting Started with Law Firm Content Marketing — 51
Content Development — 53

Developing Content — 53

Content Marketing Guidelines for Law Firms — 54
Solutions to Law Firm Content Marketing: Setting up a Department — 54

Key Takeaway — 57

Niche — 58

Define your Audience — 58

Content Distribution: Choose your Channels — 59
Content Promotion: — 59

Strategy Evaluation — 60
End Note: — 60

Chapter Four — 62

Search Engine Optimization of your law firm website for local search — 62
INTRODUCTION — 62

Directories Submission — 65

Google My Business — 66
ILLUSTRATION — 67

Quality Link Building — 68

Social Media Integration — 69

Press Releases on Local Sites and Publishers — 70

Local Keyword Targeting — 70
Conclusion — 71

Chapter Five — 72

Using LinkedIn to Market your Law Firm or Law Practice ... 72
  INTRODUCTION ... 72
  How Can LinkedIn be Useful for Your Law Firm? ... 74
  Law Firms That Use LinkedIn ... 75
  Top Tips on Using LinkedIn to Market your Law Practice/Firm ... 76
    Build a Great LinkedIn Profile: ... 77
  Creating Content: Consistently Provide High-Quality Content ... 79
    LinkedIn Video Tips: ... 80
  Your Law Firm Profile ... 83

Chapter Six ... 84
  Use of Content Aggregators and Article Directories ... 84
    INTRODUCTION ... 84
  Why Should My Law Firm Use Content Aggregators? ... 85
  Choosing the Best Platform for your Legal Content ... 86
    Setting a Budget ... 87
  Measuring ROI and other Metrics ... 89

Chapter Seven ... 90
  Adapting Specific Strategies ... 90
    INTRODUCTION ... 90
    Story for Illustration ... 91
  Localizing Your Strategies ... 93
    SWOT Analysis ... 95
  The Localization Process ... 97

Chapter Eight ... 99
  Advice ... 99
    Advice for Lawyers ... 99
  Story Point ... 100
  Referral Sources ... 101

Advice for Law Firms _____ 103
   Case Study 1_____ 106
   Case Study 2_____ 109
   Key Takeaway _____ 111

Plotting an Exit Strategy: Define your Successor _____ 112
   Lack of Succession Planning in Law Firms_____ 116
   Nigerian Law Firms are Not Designed for Differentiated Branding
   _____ 117

Planning Long Term Succession Strategy _____ 118

Choosing Firm leaders _____ 119

Succession Planning _____ 120

Challenges _____ 121

The Business of Law_____ 122

Choosing a Law Firm Business Model: Which Route to Go?
_____ 123

What Law Firms Founders Fail to Do _____ 126
   They Fail To Plan The Law Firm As a Business: _____ 126
   Growth Plan _____ 129
   Institutionalization _____ 130
   The Swiss Verein Model _____ 134

Bonus Sections _____ *137*

Becoming a Better Legal Marketer: It is your Duty _____ 138
   A Scenario _____ 140
   The Mantra _____ 141

Managing the Fee Earners_____ 144
   Review your Staff over the Years. _____ 144
   COMPENSATION OF ATTORNEYS _____ 144
   FIRM CULTURE _____ 146

Helping the Client Win _____ 149
   The Future of Work _____ 150
   How Does Multiple Skills help a Lawyer? _____ 151

Ditching the Entitlement Mentality: No One Owes you Anything _____ 155
   The Problem_____ 156
   The Marketing Aversion _____ 158

Conclusion _____ **161**
About the Author _____ *163*

Preface

Beyond merely being a good lawyer, I believe that you have to understand the way things work behind the scenes in law firm operations in order to have a well-rounded view of the law. From the client intake process, to business development initiatives geared towards attaining visibility, which will, in turn, increase profitability for the law firm, having a deeper and well-rounded understanding of the way the "business of law" really works will help a lawyer develop stronger skills that will help him gain a better footing in the provisions of legal services.

Because of my deep interest in business development and all things Digital, I strove to gain deeper understanding of how the System works. What do lawyers think of when they set up their websites? Why do they think they need to develop massive visibility so that they can gain top-of-mind awareness from prospects and potential clients out there? Do they understand how they can actively monitor their online portfolios which may encompass various listings in different directories and also involved third parties reviewing them online?

The deeper I dug, the more I realized many lawyers were floundering around and did not know what to do or how to go about setting up strong digital footprints for themselves. Sadly, a lot of them don't even know how to market themselves in a saturated marketplace oozing with other lawyers and hostile clients. Many are terrified of marketing themselves because being visible will make them open to criticism, and many people don't like being criticized for the work they do. It is like wanting to sprint across a rain-drenched field but not wanting to be touched by the rain.

My fingers got to working on this book, one keystroke at a time, page after page. I began sharing my perspective, and from there I built a narrative: that the problem of many lawyers is both ignorance and inaction—ignorance because they are not equipped with the knowledge they need to develop their book of business and build visibility, inaction because many who know this seem to be frozen down in an icy lake of inaction.

So, please enjoy this book. But while enjoying it, note one important factor: you are not reading for reading sake. Read to add to your body of knowledge. Read to act. There are questions in this book that requires deep thinking and critical answers. Keep a pen and paper beside you; jot down points and questions that come up as you read, then chew on them the way you would a legal brief.

The clock is ticking. Let's go.

Chapter One

Professional Service Firms: The Legal Services Industry in Focus

Professional service firms are an integral part of the Knowledge Economy. From lawyers, to investment bankers, to accounting firms, to consulting companies (think McKinsey & Co. and other leading global consulting firms), to risk management consultants, to management consultants, we have to agree that professional services firms are a core part of the World. However, in this little book, we are not focusing on the myriad of professional services types there are; our core focus is on lawyers and the way the provision of legal services has evolved over the past several years.

Everyone will agree that the legal services industry is a *knowledge Intensive Service* sector because of the specialized, highly technical services they (we) provide to clients. From the highly volatile world of commercial litigation, to other specific types of litigation in law Courts, to Probate practise and Estate Management, to those working within the Capital Markets, to Mergers & Acquisitions and Corporate Restructuring, to general corporate-commercial and company secretarial services, lawyers will agree that they are in a narrow niche. This narrow niche still broadens out into several micro niches, some of which require a higher level of technical know-how, expertise, and specialization.

Because of all the above, lawyers were ultra conservative. Furthermore, they didn't (don't) bother with the issue of the management of their businesses. This is even more glaring because lawyers don't have economic background, so they believe that their sole focus should be on the provision of high-quality client service for their clientele. Given these factors, many lawyers were (and are still) comfortable sitting back and waiting for clients to come to their office doorsteps. In the past, this approach may have worked because prospects had no choice; however, times have changed.

The legal services industry has been effectively disrupted. Alternative legal services providers are springing up on the Web and the World Wide Web lacks physical limitations; thus effectively evading jurisdictions where such may be completely unacceptable. Many global law firms with international focus are encroaching on territories by setting up member Firms in other jurisdictions. Given the fact that many of these top Firms are structured with profitability in mind, they usually and effectively disrupt the local legal services providers because they are at the top of their marketing game.

There are DIY websites that help their "customers" with design templates for any type of legal and commercial agreements they want. There are online alternative web providers that give clients the option of going to the gatekeepers of the legal services industry; lawyers. Furthermore, there are also more lawyers per client area than there was in the past. What this means is that there are many more lawyers now than there were in the past.

Thus, the need to become more economically profitable in the long run has become more glaring. Lawyers have to scamper for briefs in many cases. Ambulance chasing is on the rise. Now more than ever, lawyers have seen the need for the marketing of their services, within the bounds of jurisdictional limitations and Guidelines, of course.

The need for marketing has never become more glaring now than it was in the past. Sadly, the legal services industry is one industry that is not structured for competition; it is structured to make the practitioners conservative in thinking. The structure is rapidly changing. Law firms are restructuring themselves and moving into non-traditional legal areas: they are becoming estate planners or investment advisors. They are entering into the Stock markets and several other non-niche areas: immigration consulting, brand management and other consulting areas. Many are now restructuring as consultancies which is what they weren't, and while law firms cannot put together a sign that says "hire us because we win almost all our cases" because of local law prohibitions, public relations and other subtle forms of advertising are coming into play to help them deepen market share and gain more clients.

Industry Torn Apart?

What is the future of work? Sitting behind a well-worn mahogany desk, curtains on the windows pulled back to let in the evening air, while a distinguished back is bent over a legal document, poring over its contents? Or, sitting behind a MacBook (or other computer apparatus), fingers flying over the keyboard while the attorney in question is creating a legal opinion on an estate planning exercise? Or, interfacing with lawyers spread across different states in a video conference call to handle a complicated client brief?

The older crop of lawyers in the legal profession across the world—but we shall focus on Nigeria here—will agree that there is a change in the practice of the legal profession now than there was in the distant past. Lawyers would have gone all out on marketing their practices if not for express local laws that prohibits such; but does it really matter? Many jurisdictions have gotten to understand the change in the tide of the profession and allow marketing and advertising within set guidelines. Others still prohibit advertising expressly though there are ways to circumvent the rules, bend them a little to suit each Firm's marketing needs. That way, they can effectively get in front of their target audience while still conforming to local Regulations and Guidelines that regulate their marketing conduct.

Law firms in Nigeria are still expressly prohibited from advertising, but some time ago, a law firm in Lekki Lagos took out a Google Adwords campaign that allowed the firm's website to be displayed at the top of search engines alongside organic search engine results. The ads were similarly displayed on website pages that utilize the Google AdSense platform for revenue. This led to arguments and questions amongst Nigerian legal practitioners, many asking if such was allowed within the Rules of Professional Conduct for Legal Practitioners in Nigeria. Some argued for and against. While all agreed that advertising is expressly forbidden (yes, in Nigeria, attorneys are not allowed to market their practice), some took the line that the times have changed and lawyers would have to change with it. The people in the latter category agreed that the practise of taking out Google Adwords for a law firm website to appear alongside organic search results was never envisaged within the Rules for Legal Practitioners, so it didn't matter. And even if it did matter, they argued, it went more to show the state of law practice: that the Times have changed and the profession will have to change along with it.

Furthermore, as an addition to the events of recent times and the fact that the legal services industry across the world what it was in the past, Technology also entered the equation. Technology is no longer a phenomenon like it was in the past but an integral part of operations for professionals, lawyers included. However, in keeping with the supposed conservative nature of the profession, many lawyers are expressly against the use of tech.

Many lawyers prefer sitting back and writing their briefs in long hand for it to be subsequently typed up by a secretary while the 21st century crop of Gen Y and Z lawyers and paralegals prefer moving their fingers with blithering speed across their keyboards to get the work done swiftly and move on. Many law firms have moved on into exploring ways total automation of processes can help them work through their work load so as to increase time spent on work and maximize efficiency.

- The increasing importance of the Internet and tech in general in communications across different sectors has redefined the knowledge space.

- There is now a large access to information which could not be easily gotten — and in some cases were completely inaccessible — and softwares that enable the conglomeration of large amounts of information and data sets for retrieval and usage, including for non-technical persons.

- The Internet has created a level playing field for lawyers across board, whether they're practitioners with 20 years post qualification experience or 2 years PQE, particularly in terms of creating visibility for their practices.

All these have left a traditional, rigid profession in disruption. New practice areas have emerged, and all these emerging practice areas require the practitioners to be extremely tech-savvy and have more than a passing acquaintance with the Digital sphere. Areas like Blockchain and Smart Contracts are new areas that require use of tech to navigate through them.

The drum beats that will accompany this chapter are more distinctly martial than romantic, more battle-tilted than rose-tinted, because the situation is massively chaotic and gets even more so by the day. The profession is in turmoil. Newer, sleeker law firms are moving like Ninjas through the legal Night, slashing and cutting down their older counterparts with an arsenal of weapons that their older counterparts probably never knew existed.

Marketing is martial, rendered even more so when jurisdictions like Nigeria place stilts on them.

And these raise important questions that require some answers: what then is the future? How can lawyers and law firms navigate through this future? What will work and will not work?

Let's find out, shall we?

Chapter Two

Building a Digital Presence: The Importance of Having Online Portfolios

INTRODUCTION

Law firms have gotten to understand that they have to gain visibility for the services they are offering to potential clients. To that effect, a law firm website that is well designed and professional-looking has the capability to attract the attention of potential clients and have them contacting your law firm for their services needs. Many law firms that do not have websites that can serve as their 2/7 sales person are looking for solutions on how to key into Digital for their practises.

In the old days of law practice, a lawyer or law firm would need several years of practice in order to gain a strong foothold and become attractive to potential clients who are interested in their practice areas. However, the same is not the case today: the Internet has rendered everyone to become global citizens, meaning that even an attorney with barely a month's practice under his legal belt can gain more visibility and attract more clients online than an attorney or law firm that has over a decade practice but who/which has little to no visibility. The Internet has placed everyone on an equal footing because the same resources can be accessed by everyone.

Now, there is more to running a successful law practice than having a fancy physical office address and having your contact details out there in the Yellow Pages. You also need to have a web address; an online presence that will serve as your sales manager who's active, 24/7 and who is accessible from all corners of the world.

Nowadays, people start their search online. If someone has a legal issue or thinks that he does, the first thing he/she does is to conduct an online search. That part is extremely important for them. They could be looking for information on their pending divorce, or they may be looking to take out a long-term mortgage, or they're looking to start a business in Lagos or Abuja or wherever else. Whatever it is, they need information. They search for information that can help them on that journey; it is important to note this: *they are not merely looking for information on which attorneys would be a good fit. They are searching for usable information.*

So, that's where your website and thought leadership positioning comes to play. What do you have on your site? What are you offering? How does the prospective client perceive that you can solve their problem for which they are looking for legal advice or legal representation? How does your online portfolio present you to your prospect?

Many lawyers believe that they need a web presence, but they don't seem to know precisely how to go about this or what precisely to do. Many think it is all about keyword research and stuffing of those keywords around their websites. Many cannot differentiate between prospects and users who are information gatherers and those who're ready for action with regards to their legal situation. The situation is simple: you may be unable to pinpoint the level each prospect is in their buyer journey and the closer they are to buying, the higher the possibility that they will contact you if they feel you possess the answers to their problems or that you understand their situation enough to be able to do something legally about it.

In this section, we will break the information down.

Website Design for your Legal Practice

In the past, lawyers had no online marketing options. Outside Nigeria, lawyers could use the Yellow Pages and take out ads in newspapers. With the development of, and expansion of the Internet, lawyers deviated from the traditional marketing platforms towards having their own practice websites to serve as their online interface accessible to the whole world.

Basics to Note:

- A professionally designed law firm website is your online address and can retain the attention of your law firm website visitors.

- Your law firm website will help you gain credibility in the eyes of your prospects who land on your website from different areas of the Internet.

- Your law firm website will help your law firm to increase their conversion rates in the sales funnel and turn prospects to paying clients when the time is right.

- Your website address is your sales person, available 24/7 to help you convert leads and gain visibility to colleagues and potential clients who may be interested in utilizing whatever services your firm offers.

- Your law firm website is not an end in and of itself; it is merely a tool which ought to be sharpened and used well in order to maximize benefits that will accrue from it.

- The website is the central repository of information about your law firm and its practitioners. It is safer to ensure that all relevant information is available on the site.

- A website does not sleep unlike lawyers and other professionals who have to sleep after a hard day's work. Having this marketing tool will ensure that interested will always be able to interact with your online portfolio.

- It is a powerful marketing tool that you should *never* overlook. *Ever*.

Law Firm Website Preparation

Before delving into creating a law firm website, there are certain basics you must cover. There is more to setting up a law firm website than merely slapping a homepage, an About Us and a Contact Page together. Thoughtful planning must be put into the creation of your law firm site and you need to let your creative/design firm be aware of this. Ordinarily they should, but it helps if you understand the rudiments of what your law firm website should look like and how they should go about it. It helps if you have an idea in mind of what you want and your team will help you implement it.

An in-house team would make more sense. The reason is simple: your law firm website is not something you can just open and then abandon on the World Wide Web. Things don't happen that way. Search Engine Optimization is important. Thought leadership is important. News/press releases from your law firm's press room is extremely important too. Please note that law firms are becoming full press rooms with massive content they can churn out to their audience. Is that something you can effectively outsource by putting a creative agency on retainer? Or do you think you would be better off with an in-house IT team handling your law firm website from within? Whichever you think is better, no problem. Utilize it. But you have to absolutely note that your law firm website is not something that can be *just* abandoned once it's been created. That's a sure recipe for disaster and a dip in search engine rankings.

Law Firm Website Pages Planning

When creating a law firm website, it is paramount that you create your law firm website pages concept map before you begin its implementation. Drawing your website pages outline will help you to know precisely what you are developing for the website and how to link them all up through internal hyperlinks. You can draw that up using a design tool on your computer, or you can get a long sheet and do that physically. Personally, I prefer the latter, with the sheet spread out on a floor, my pencil flying over it to add the necessary pages and create linking lines to show the structure they'll take when the design process begins. Please consider the following:

- Homepage
- Areas of Practise
- About Us
- Contact and Location
- Client Testimonials
- Publications
- Press Releases
- Attorneys
- Case Studies
- Any other pages/areas you feel your website should have.

When you have drawn up the above, then congratulations, you have drawn your sitemap and you are ready to proceed to the next step. Note that they won't take the form above; it's just to give you an idea of what to do.

Please note that your law firm site map mustn't follow the structure above. The above is merely for illustration purposes to give you and your design team an idea of what they can come up with. You have to note your own unique circumstances and law practice, plus note the applicable Regulations in your jurisdiction on Attorney advertising when drawing up your site map. This should take some soul-searching, but it shouldn't be too complicated.

Crafting Content for your Law Firm Website Pages

With your law firm sitemap ready, you have to create the proper content that will go with each page, starting from the website's homepage. When creating content, you have to consider the type of page each one is and know if there are any additional add-ons that will accompany them like images, graphics, videos, etc. Also note that the content marketer/copywriter will write the content with localized SEO in mind.

Law Firm Website Design Evaluation

You choose the design elements you want to use [or your developer does that for you] and then you evaluate same to ensure that it is suited to your needs. Fonts, colors, spacing, everything that will go into the website should be evaluated at this point. You have to also note that your website outlook should go in line with your Branding imagery and logo so as to make for a consistent branding outlook for everything you are doing.

Integral Points to Note About Your Law Firm Website Design

Navigation:

Your law firm website should have intuitive navigation and should be easy for even the biggest Internet novice to find themselves around the core pages of your law firm website and find these areas in your law firm website:

Your services

Your attorneys

Your Contact information and Phone numbers

Your core values

Your law firm's case studies

Your law firm's thought leadership which will encompass its areas of expertise.

Click-To-Call

Individual Pages Law firm websites should contain the firm's contact phone number so that visitors to the site can find it easy to call the law firm contact handles with the press of a button. Many law firm websites bears these click-to-call phone numbers at the header of each page so that all users have to do is to click on the number as they navigate through the website so that they can get in touch immediately with the contact person of the law firm and discuss their needs.

Most people browse through the Internet with their mobile devices, and chances are, they will call you on their mobile devices as well. So, leaving the law firm's phone number in a conspicuous space on your law firm website will be beneficial to prospects seeking to call the law firm directly from the website. It will definitely be better than hiding the phone numbers away on a page the prospects will have to start searching for if they need to contact your law firm.

Call-to-Action/Lead Generation Forms

Every professional website needs a lead generation form. Some would prefer to use the term contact form. Some prefer to have lead generation forms across multiple pages of their site, preferably in the practice area pages of their websites.

As part of their strategy, some law firms also include their lead generation forms in the thought leadership pages of their law firm website, prompting readers to get in touch with them and setting actionable steps they can take to do that. Whichever one you want to call it, or however placement you want your lead generation forms to have, there are certain basics you have to take notice of:

It has to be easy. You have to ensure that the information needed from the potential client at that point is merely basic. Ideally, potential clients on your law firm website should have to fill these: their name, contact info and email address, and a brief summary of why they are contacting you for their needs. Anything more should be shelved for either when the prospect is facing your attorneys in a meeting or when you are making a follow-up of the contact. It doesn't have to be too detailed so your prospects don't feel too pressed for information, but it has to cover the basics. Every other information needed will have to wait for your initial phone or face-to-face consultation.

The point is that you are not going to, or trying to, close the prospect right there on your lead generation pages. The goal is gather enough information as would enable you to get in touch with the prospect and effectively pitch your firm's legal services to them.

Use Compelling Headlines for Your Practice Areas

There are several law firm practice areas; you already know the practice areas you are targeting. They could be the areas you already work in or want to break into over the course of time. You also know the practice areas your law firm practitioners address and the sectors targeted. Use compelling headlines and sub-headings to explain your practice area expertise across each of your law firm website's practice areas. Headlines are important because they present to the reader in precise, popping terms the content of the page they are navigating into/through. Point to note:

Unique Value Proposition: Your unique value proposition for your law firm prospects must be easy to glean from whatever page they are navigating through. At a glance, your law firm website visitor has to understand the value your law firm is proposing to them and how you intend to deliver that value to them. Make this as perfectly clear as possible.

Slapping together marketing catch phrases you don't even believe may be too easy to spot in the long run. In legal marketing, you have to remember to communicate your core values to potential clients, and it must be easy to shine for prospects to take note of.

Content

The whole internet has agreed that content is king. Whether it is static content, or long articles, or blog posts that are geared towards making people understand your subject matter expertise, content is important for any website. There are no two words about it.

There are different forms of content, and there are different categories of audiences that each content form will appeal to. While some will be happier swiftly zapping through an infographic, another will be all too happy to read a long form article of three thousand words, and another will go for a technical article on a specific niche.

Your law firm content could take any form. It could be videos, podcasts, blog posts, long form articles, infographics. They are all content. If your law firm can develop a content marketing strategy and follow it through on their website, then the benefits are enormous. First is that search engines like Google will have something to crawl through when their bots visit your law firm website to crawl for content to index. Second is that your law firm website will rank for more keywords on the Search Engine Result Pages.

There is an important point to note: When people have legal issues they need answers to, the very first thing they generally do is to go online to search for answers. If these people who need these answers—and their problems form part of your law firm practice areas—come upon your law firm's informative content on your website, they can also seek your services out for solutions to their legal problems.

Content creation and marketing opens up your law firm's Brand to visitors who are perusing through the vast infinity of the Internet, there is no doubt about that. It also has the capability of showcasing your law firm to be a subject matter expert in a specific law practice niche, say Private Client & Offshore Advisory. And all these are beneficial to your law firm. They can help your law firm convert your visitors into paying clients. We shall dedicate another chapter to content marketing.

Case Studies

These are proof-of-service. They are signals that you have done the work you showcase as part of your law firm's service expertise. Creating case studies of your law firm's past work experience on your law firm website is actual proof that you have service experience in the areas of expertise you claim you have on your law firm website. By analyzing the work you have done for clients in the past [within the bounds you are able to disclose per your Bar ethics codes and client agreements], you are showing potential clients that you have done the type of work they may need in the past, which means you have experience in that area and can do it again for them.

Technical Points to Note for Your Law Firm website

Website Speed

The speed of your law firm's website is extremely important. Any website that has slow loading times is definitely off-putting for any user and they will click out of the web site with the same speed they clicked into it. Kissmetrics has estimated that slow-loading websites suffer a lot, and the reason is simple: your users expect your law firm website to load within 3 seconds flat. Anything longer is a waste of their time and will increase your website's bounce rate. And when your website's bounce rate is going on the high side, Google will take notice and conclude that your website is not delivering value for search users when they enter your website through the Google SERPs.

What could be causing your law firm website's slow loading times? It could be heavy, uncompressed images that load simultaneously with the page, or graphics that bog down the page being loaded. Or it could be due to the use of too many plugins; these can also affect a website loading speed. Whatever it is, try to find out. For images, you can enable lazy loading images. Just note that you have to bear in mind that there are several factors that can lag your law firm website loading speed; whatever they are, you have to ensure that you make them disappear so that your website can be as fast as possible.

SSL Certificates

SSL (Secure Socket Locator) Certificates are scripts that show that your website is secure. It is identified by the https prefix that comes before your law firm website address at the address bar of the Internet browser used by your site visitors. If your website has SSL Certificates installed, then the https sign is shown on the top leftmost side of the address bar in the form of a green-colored padlock. SSL certificates is important for your law firm website, particularly if your law firm's website has client log-in areas through which your law firm clients can log into the law firm portal and access their case files and other important aspects of their cases with your law firm.

Taking Action for your Law Firm Website

You now have an idea of what your law firm website should include and perhaps how it should be structured, so it is time to take action. If you are still lost, then sit back, pick up a pen and deeply ruminate. Ask yourself these questions: what are the law firms practising in your local area that you admire? Or, what are the top law firms in your jurisdiction? Do they have websites? (I will bet my entire professional practice that they do). Do you like the design, layout and content of their website? If you do, would you consider having a similar design for your law firm website? If you don't, what *precisely* don't you like? What would you prefer?

Have a very clear expectation in your mind which you can easily communicate to your design firm or in-house creative team. By having an idea of precisely what you want, you can then know precisely how to have your design team structure your law firm website. Taking notes of all these can help in creating a very definite guide in the mind as to precisely what your law firm wants for its online needs.

Remember: first impressions matter with people, and your law firm website may be the first point of contact a prospect is going to have with your law firm before making their decision to either call in or consider hiring you to service their needs. Or, they may have no needs, but the contents of your law firm website so wowed them that they dolled out their email to you. Bingo! You scored a point. If the website is not easy to navigate, or that the site is not optimized for mobile devices, then you have a losing one on your hands.

Chapter Three

Law Firm Content Marketing: A New Marketing Guide

INTRODUCTION

Lawyers are trained professionally to be lawyers. They're not trained to be anything else. This means that many lawyers fail to understand business development. Many don't understand the concept of business development and don't care. Others understand what the concept is in relation to their law practise but are at a loss as to how to go about it. Ask a lawyer to write you an article, and chances are, when they present the article to you, you'll feel as you're reading through a bulky brief of argument even though you're merely reading through an article. Chances are too, you don't make sense of what you are reading because it may feel too dense for your understanding, considering that you are not a lawyer or paralegal. They are probably trained to think *and* write like lawyers, so there.

In this chapter, the focus is on law firm content marketing. How can you market your law firm or law practice (if you are a solo practitioner) using content? How can you make people trust your knowledge? How will you be able to deliver content that resonates with your potential clients and have them trust your judgment? What form will your content take if and when you decide to start?

If you are part of your law firm's marketing team and you are reading this chapter, you will probably make more sense out of it than a lawyer since they're trained to handle the Law and you are trained to market them to the world. Some lawyers are actually quite savvy and can make sense out of this; plus, they know and understand how to navigate their way around the digital world.

Content marketing is for everyone, including conservative professionals like lawyers. Top performing law firms in the world utilize content as part of their marketing efforts, and it pays off. Reason: content is one of the most effective ways of getting and retaining a readership base, possibly converting them into paying clients in the sales funnel when the time is right.

Remember that in spite of all's said and done, content remains King.

For the lawyers that even make the effort to post stuff on social media, including firms, all many of them do is to merely post news of their attendance at different events. Lawyers are versatile and usually know a lot of people, which ultimately means that they attend lots of events. They post no takeaways, no useful information beyond the occurrence of the event itself. In many cases, lawyers do speak at these events and they cover topics professionals who could not attend would love to learn more about. However, they don't expand that attendance at those events and their keynoting sessions into educative thought leadership that will keep their audience hooked to their Brand.

Many law firms also post about their associates being seconded to foreign law firms or international organizations. The news is usually almost always bland and focuses on *them*. They *don't* focus on their potential legal services consumer. Because of this, the firm's social media, SEO and thought leadership all suffer in the long run because their pages are filled with information about *them*.

Key Takeaway: Legal services consumers are not interested in being informed that one of your associates working in Lagos was seconded to the Johannesburg offices of White & Case LLP. They are also not interested in reading about a fancy event some of your Firm associates attended. What they are interested in is finding out how your law firm can help them solve problems. The problems could be business related, or contentious issues that may lead to litigation—they need to learn how your expertise can be deployed to help them make their problems go away. Never forget that.

What is Content Marketing?

Content marketing is a strategic content plan created and implemented by businesses with a view to educating readers (who are also potential customers and clients) and converting them into customers and clients when the time is right in the sales process. Content marketing helps creative professionals display their thought leadership positioning in an industry and also market themselves for their professional practice.

By consistently providing top, stellar content for your law firm blog readers, you establish your Firm and Practice as a subject matter expert in a specific area you are targeting. You're creating confidence in the mind of your readers and making them consider your law firm a trustworthy source of valuable information for their knowledge needs. If and when they need information in the future, they will probably look to your law firm's educational materials for knowledge. If they need assistance, they may look to your Firm for solutions.

Sadly, many lawyers tend to overlook content marketing as an integral part of their law firm marketing playbook, choosing instead to focus on other marketing activities. For many, this is borne out of the irrational fear that releasing content out into the deep world of the Internet Ether means that they are giving away their "secret sauce"; they are giving away their highly technical information for free to people who should ordinarily have to come to the doors of their law firm to consult them for their knowledge on the issues they're facing.

I understand this fear. I used to have that same fear. However, I have joined the few marketers that hold the view that information should be given out freely to the entire world if and when they need it. The thing is that some people just want to be educated on a specific area and they won't use it in the future. Others are looking for information but will be unable to execute what they have learned themselves—that is where you come in. Execution becomes the end result of your efforts.

Examples of Popular Law Blogs

JD Supra

Mondaq

Lexology

Note that these three are legal content providers that aggregate content from hundreds of member law firms in different jurisdictions so that readers can read their content and resonate with their value offerings. Still, it means that member firms submitting to these three content aggregators are in the content marketing game, creating valuable knowledge-based content on diverse areas of the Law like Mergers & Acquisitions, Intellectual Property & Brand Protection, Private Client & Offshore matters, Commercial Litigation, etc. They're setting themselves up as experts in that area for the positive perception of their readers, and they succeed.

Furthermore, they are buying into the existing subscription base of these content aggregators, which means that they will have thousands of readers ready to read their content if they choose to publish with these aggregators. The point is simply that these content aggregators have a large number of people who are their target audience as their subscribers, so they push their content out to them to reach those readers directly.

We have digressed and will look at content aggregators later.

Developing a Law Firm Content Marketing Strategy

Content marketing is not all about creating content; you also have to develop a strategy for it. It is imperative that your Law Firm's business development/marketing team develops an editorial calendar for your law firm's content marketing efforts. They should also develop a content marketing strategy. The reason is simply because it is always better to set down a specific vision on paper and then take the appropriate steps to see it through. So, if you've been creating random blog posts, stop! Create a calendar, then follow it through on a monthly basis.

A new law firm which has streamlined its practice into niche areas of the Law should also have little to no difficulty coming up with a content marketing strategy that can be executed over the long term and modified if and when the need arises. A law firm that has an idea of the type of clientele it wants for its practice should have no difficulty developing a content marketing calendar in that area to service the needs of their proposed clientele. A law firm that has a team with a non-technical mindset would probably be on track in developing their strategy.

The overriding point to note when developing a content marketing calendar is that it has to be focused on addressing the pain points of the client base of the law firm in question. This is imperative. Your law firm content should never be all about you and your team; it should be all about addressing the sector areas your (potential) clients operate in and showing them that you can address their pain points.

What Do Clients Want?

It is important to answer this question. The answer to the above question is key to understanding the type of strategy to develop and the editorial calendar that can be in line with the developed strategy for execution. Sadly, this question: "What do Clients Want?" is one that has no clear answer.

The economy is bleak. Problems beset every facet of the economy. Trade disputes erupt from all corners. Clients are getting increasingly sophisticated and will not tolerate bad service or bad content from their service providers. If one provider seems to be under delivering or does not live up to expectations, they will be changed at the drop of a hat. So, what do clients really want? What type of content would they want to read?

Sadly, many lawyers are completely clueless about the type of content their prospective clients or their already existing client base would like to read from them which makes them to churn out content that reads like legal briefs. Unfortunately, clients do not want to read legal briefs from attorneys; they are too technical, laced with layers upon layers of legal arguments that are designed to sway the thinking of a seasoned legal mind to their line of argument. To make it even more unbearable, they are *long* and *boring* to wade through, and clients/readers have no time for that. Their attention span is too short, sadly. They need to be swiftly serviced.

Now, the same time-honored and under-answered questions again: what do clients want?

Before developing a content marketing strategy and editorial style guide that will be followed through the firm's marketing materials, a law firm may conduct a survey. This may sound shocking to some people, but it may be imperative in the long run to do this so that the editorial decision is served by the precise editorial needs of their proposed client base. Knowing with precision what non-legal readers would like to read would go a long way in developing the type of content that they would like to read in the long run from the law firm.

Furthermore, when looking at the pain points readers may wish to see addressed through informative content, it will make a lot of sense to dig into the legal issues clients face which necessitate them seeking out professional legal help. This will provide deep insights to what the editorial team will need to look out when creating their content.

Benefits of having a Law Firm Content Marketing Strategy

The benefits of content marketing for all types of businesses cannot be overemphasized. If your law firm can develop a content marketing strategy and follow it through, the benefits are enormous. Data has shown that people first go online when they have an issue. If people who may need your law firm's service offerings search for answers to their legal problems and come upon your law firm's informative content, there is every chance they will go for you to provide their solutions.

Content creation and marketing opens up your law firm's brand to visitors, there is no doubt about that. It also has the capability of showcasing your law firm to be a subject matter expert in a specific law practice niche, say Private Client & Offshore Advisory. And all these are beneficial to your law firm. They can help your law firm convert your visitors into paying clients.

Getting Started with Law Firm Content Marketing

The very first step would be to develop and align a Firm-wide strategy. This is extremely important. A strategy will help your law firm focus its attention on what it wants to achieve. Your team members and Firm practitioners will each know their role in the overall effort. In some firms, they leave the content marketing to the in-house team; some firms outsource their content marketing needs to content marketing agencies that work with the legal services industry. Whichever way, it is imperative that there is an alignment of goals between the content marketing team and the working fee earners. Content is not really about churning out content, but creating content that will resonate with the firm's target audience and answer their in-depth questions about the legal issues they would like to see addressed by the law firm. Many professionals (lawyers included) have the opinion that it would be detrimental to the increase of their clientele base if they keep giving away their technical knowledge on blogs and articles and podcasts. However, this is far from the truth. Research has shown that prospective clients usually first seek out general information on the legal issue they would like to see address before contacting a Firm; it makes the onboarding process less cumbersome if they know what to expect in their consultation with a law firm. Furthermore, for every firm that decides that they cannot give away their technical legal knowledge and analysis of legal issues for free, there are thousands of firms out there who are already working aggressively in that regard, hoping to capture the attention of prospects online through their content marketing efforts.

Content Development

Your law firm marketing team will have this question to ask themselves: what type of content can we develop for our readers?

The type of content to develop is definitely varied, and can cover several areas of Law and legal pain points which your clients generally encounter. A law firm that has twenty years experience handling client issues will have no problem coming up with a content marketing strategy for their content marketing team because they would have already seen and handled a lot of issues for clients in the past. This will give them an idea of what clients are facing, which will in turn influence their editorial guidelines for their content marketing drive.

Developing Content

They could take these forms: long form articles, opinion articles (on different legal issues and even court judgments), blog posts, case studies, legal series that focus on specific areas of the Law, podcasts, and even Video. The list is diverse and it is up to your law firm marketing team to make their choice. Some will choose to utilize a diverse array of formats for their content marketing while some will be comfortable sticking to one or two formats and dominating them rather than spreading their efforts too wide.

Content Marketing Guidelines for Law Firms

Here, the focus is on how leading law firms can leverage content marketing and how they can streamline their content marketing efforts by their marketing department. These strategies outlined below will help a law firm in creating their content marketing team and editorial calendar.

Solutions to Law Firm Content Marketing: Setting up a Department

Hire in-house writers

Many law firms hire great writers to craft their law firm content for them so that potential clients can see their thought leadership. They hire great social media specialists and consultants who can craft great content. However, there is a problem with this: law is a highly technical area and it will require either someone with a 1st degree in Law or a lawyer to deeply understand the workings of the Law well enough to write something reasonable from it.

If the law firm has an in-house content specialist to work in the firm's media and communications department, it is imperative that the person hired understands the workings of the Law or is a lawyer. That way, it will be easier for the person to handle the various practise area expertise of the law firm and convert them into great thought leadership posts. It is fantastic to note that some lawyers combine law practise with writing, while some lawyers transit from full-time law practise to legal marketing—they will surely have the capacity to handle content for law firms that need their services.

Hiring External Content Specialists

For law firms that do not have the option to hire in-house content marketers to work with their teams, they can opt for hiring external content marketers to work with the firm so as to produce high-quality thought leadership content for the firm's social media, company pages and other digital assets.

The great thing about choosing this option is that there are many young lawyers who are fabulous writers and who have the zeal to handle editorial work for law firms. Furthermore, there are also content marketing specialists that work exclusively with law firms and the legal services industry generally. They are content gurus, with great social media and marketing experience, and many have served as consultants to law firms and legal marketing departments either across the country or across the world. In my own case I am an attorney and external consultant, advising law firms, with the aim of devising their marketing strategies to reach their potential clientele base across their chosen target audience.

Personally, I think that the best thing a law firm can do if it is interested in making good work with content is to have a seasoned writer/attorney handle it. The reason is simple: the person is an attorney and would definitely understand the workings of the Law without needing an extra mental push. Furthermore, creating content that resonates with readers is a priority for such a person because of the person's deep understanding of storytelling techniques. This creates a double advantage: having in-depth knowledge of the workings of the Law and also having story telling expertise that can be leveraged to reach potential target audiences.

Key Takeaway

Law firm content marketing is more difficult than content marketing for other consulting spheres and practises because of the difficulty that exists in not identifying the interests of potential clients, but also crafting thought leadership posts that are geared towards actively educating them on their problems, while at the same time proffering solutions to these problems. Potential clients need to have a degree of confidence in the law firm before they can choose that law firm for their legal service needs if and when the need for legal service arises.

It is also instructive to note that lawyers will surely write superior content on issues bordering on the law than any layman ever can or will. Furthermore, in spite of this seemingly uplifting news, a lawyer with content marketing and/or digital marketing training who has an insightful understanding of the needs of clients with the added ability to possibly think like them, will provide better strategy and content than a lawyer who merely relies only on his skill in the letters of the Law.

Niche

Your law firm will have to choose the niche areas it wishes to write on. For a law firm that exclusively handles commercial transactions, it will definitely be better for such a law firm to target its content marketing efforts at creating articles and content in that subject area. For a general-practice law firm, a more diverse approach will be beneficial. The law firm marketing team can then split this up according to practise area and assign the content creation to the relevant attorneys that work within those areas or who're interested in researching into those areas. With each attorney coming up with a sheet of client questions within their areas of legal practise, it will be easier for the law firm content marketing team to come up with the relevant content strategy and follow same through, working in line with the different practise niches the law firm attorneys work in.

Define your Audience

This is quite necessary. Your law firm marketing team should create the ideal buyer persona you are developing your articles for. Create a hypothetical profile detailing age, work status, legal issues and pain points, etc, that may be addressed for such a client persona. Then you plot your content marketing strategy along those lines, for that person. This is important so that you don't create random content in spite of your comprehensive content marketing plan.

Content Distribution: Choose your Channels

When you create your law firm content, where do you publish them? Do you publish them on your company website and social media pages? Where? This may prove to be a dilemma, as many law firms would not want to include blog posts in their law firm website. No problem.

You can plan your distribution channels and choose where you can publish: your law firm blog, your law firm's official company profile, Typepad, LinkedIn, etc.

Content Promotion:

While it is good to love the good old organic search traffic that your company blogs and articles may garner, it would be a good strategy to promote these contents across different channels. I love saying it thus: pay your pay to the top if you can. So, channel promotion of your law firm's content can perform wonders if done right and if targeted well. Furthermore, remember that great content is utterly useless if there is no one to read it or if it remains buried deep in the pages of your website.

Strategy Evaluation

We live in a data-driven world right now. Everything is evaluated as Data. Your law firm content should live and thrive in this world of Data, too. If you are publishing on your law firm's dedicated blog or company website, you can install certain scripts that can help you analyze your law firm's content marketing performance. To do this: I believe Google Analytics is a Wonder tool for website performance metrics analysis.

Google Analytics monitor website metrics like visitors by day, time, location, click-through rates, referral source, bounce rates, etc. These data metrics point out where your law firm content is doing well and where it's not, then the latter can be adjusted accordingly to make your content perform the way you want it to be.

End Note:

The world has changed. Marketing has changed. Content marketing and advertising has changed. In the past, lawyers were merely ministers in the temple of Justice, dispensing justice and having their living wages earned from the little money grateful clients put into their palms. In our current world, lawyers are corporate gurus and consultants offering wide, far-reaching range of services to meet the ever increasing demands of their clients.

Your law firm needs to change too in order to leverage these applicable changes for the good of your content marketing strategy.

I know that there Regulatory bottlenecks for lawyers seeking to market themselves, but there are ways to market yourself and your law practise without running afoul of these Regulations.

Chapter Four

Search Engine Optimization of your law firm website for local search

INTRODUCTION

SEO is a term every digital marketer or digital consultant is aware of. We all want our sites to rank highly for relevant, targeted keywords. What everyone seems to agree upon is that business websites should be optimized for local search queries from specific regions. This runs in line with the thinking: act local, think global. So, while agreeing that firms now target a global audience for their products and services, there is still a focus on local regional targeting of online assets in order to be discovered in the world of Search by local buyers.

For law firms that have their own web sites where they showcase their vision and thought leadership, it wouldn't make sense to merely leave the website on the Internet just for the sake of having a website. Optimizing the website for search and Local Search is important. With the massive proliferation and explosion of websites across the world, online competition has become fierce and people are forced to learn to play by new rules wherein the gatekeepers are Search Engine bots, Algorithms and other sophisticated machine learning and AI systems that aim to provide only the most relevant results for search queries by users around the Globe.

Right now, in the world of Search, Local Search is important, Ultra Localized Search, even more so. Local search can be generalized to a larger geographical construct: New York, Lagos, Abuja, London, and the list go on. These are large cities, each with their various sections and zones, streets and areas of interest. Obviously it cannot be only one or two firms that are located within them; there are usually several, perhaps in their hundreds, that dot these cities. Thus, localizing Search to merely London or Lagos will *not* cut teeth; ultra localizing the Search to specific neighbourhoods, specific areas of the cities, will make more sense.

A person searching for a law firm in Abuja or Lagos or London will not be searching for law firms within the generic City limits; their search will be tailored to the areas around the neighbourhoods where they work or where they live. The search will not be thrown out to Lagos or New York; the search will be localized to "Law firms in Anthony Lagos" or "Corporate Law firms close to Central Park" or "Lawyers in Baker Street, Lagos". A lot of people will not have the time for this, and will instead choose to search for "law firms near me" and their phone will serve up relevant results based on the searcher's GPS pinpoint of their location on their mobile phone or other Internet surfing device.

Because names like Lagos, Abuja, London, New York, and other cities around the world are "generic" names for search purposes, SEO specialists and firms are learning to localize targeting to more specific areas and streets because searchers are localizing their search to more specific areas within the larger metropolitan areas. This helps you to target people who are within direct location reach of your law firm and who may turn out to be clients in the future.

Directories Submission

There are several local directories you can submit your company's business details and website to. Most of these directories are international search directories, with local sections for each country they have directory listings for. At country-wide levels, there are great business directories that accept submissions from relevant businesses and other similar sites for listing on their directory list.

The list of directories is endless. Sortlist, Crunchbase, Hg.org, Lawyers.com, Avvo, there are several others. All these local directories (some are international, though they have country directories for country-specific listings) link back externally to your site, thus making it discoverable for people searching for law firms within their location.

These software directories usually have high search engine ranking and some of their top listings usually pop up at the top of search engine searches. That is why many businesses struggle to place their business details and website on these directories so that they can be found by people relevant to the business they do. Many law firms go as far as purchasing premium listings for annual subscriptions so that these Directories will rank their law firms listings higher in their Directories.

Google My Business

Googly My Business is Google's free localized business listing for businesses with a local physical address. If your law firm has a physical address—and most law firms do as we still usually practise more of the brick-and-mortar office location style—then it makes great sense for you to register that business location on Google My Business and use the free tool to rank on Google Search and Google Maps for searches related to your business.

For firms that have different branches with their own addresses all across the country, each of these branches of the firm can each list their different addresses on Google My Business and showcase the address, details, phone numbers, and website of the business (if the firm has one). Plus, people can leave their reviews of your business on the review section of your Google my Business listing.

Google my Business is crucial for localized search engine ranking, because people tend to search for businesses that are close to them and Google always aims to serve up the most relevant search results for their search queries.

ILLUSTRATION

I recently relocated to Victoria Island, Lagos from Johannesburg, and I am looking for a law firm near me. I type in: "Law Firms in Victoria Island". If I used Google for the search, then, on the top of the search engine results (if I had conducted the search with a mobile phone), law firms in Victoria Island Lagos who have local listings on Google my Business, will appear, along with other top-ranking results. If I click into the law firm's listing, the firm's overview, contact phone number, hours and days of operation, and other pertinent information about the firm will be revealed. From there, I can even click into the law firm's website and peruse through the content there to see if the firm has what I need. I can even choose to call the firm directly from their Google my Business listing.

So, if you are looking to rank for local Search queries for your company, then getting your business details listed on Google my Business is a requirement. Not only will your business turn up on the SERPs [search engine result pages], your business will also turn up on Google Maps and this will be great for local search via Maps. This is one of the most powerful local search optimization tools a firm can use to boost its ranking and get discovered on Search.

Quality Link Building

When you create your website content, it is important and imperative that you build internal links. Since your website is already structured around your niche areas of expertise, your content is going to reflect the same. So, when you write and publish your content on your law firm website's blog page, make sure you build links within your articles to other relevant articles within the same website. These can serve as further go-to resources within the same practise area that particular blog post dealt on.

We call these links internal links. They serve as treasure points that lead visitors to your law firm website's pages to other relevant content within your website. It also aids Google and other search engines to understand your pages and crawl them faster since these will make you rank higher for the keywords you are targeting with your link building.

When building links, your SEO team should also be mindful that they have to build external links to other high-authority sites out there that service your niche.

Social Media Integration

This issue may seem over-emphasized, but it is important to create social media profiles across the networks you feel is important for your law firm's online visibility. When you create these social media profiles for your business, you should maintain your "Brand Voice" across these other channels to ensure that you maintain the style of your Brand used on your website.

Twitter, Facebook, Instagram, Reddit, Quora, Medium, LinkedIn, and other social media platforms may be useful to your law firm. Please note that you don't have to create an account with every social media website out there; choose the ones relevant to your law firm's niche and target audience, create your profile, then populate it over time with great content. Better the choice of one or two carefully chosen social media accounts than to proliferate profiles across multiple social media sites and abandon them because you're stretching your advertising and marketing spend too thin.

When you create these social media profiles for your business, integrate them into your site. Use relevant links to showcase your social media presence. Furthermore, because these social media sites have extremely high SEO rankings, your company can be found easily if someone is searching for it on the Internet.

Press Releases on Local Sites and Publishers

Is there something happening in your business offices? Are you onboarding a new partner or research assistant? Did your company bag an award? Create a press release and have same published with reputable media outlets and websites, particularly within your physical locality and region. Create back links to your law firm's website for people who may want to find out more about your law firm.

However, don't send your press releases to spammy sites oozing with spammy links. If you do that, then not only will you be penalized when Google bots latch on to this, your site may be yanked off Google search entirely. Google is the largest search engine in the world and people use it more than any other search engine out there. Getting your law firm's website yanked from their SERPs will be disastrous to your law firm website's organic reach.

Local Keyword Targeting

If you have your offices in Lagos, it would make sense to use the key phrase "Lagos" in your pages, meta descriptions, placeholder images, and within important areas of your website. You should use these local keywords you're targeting so that search engines will have an idea of what you are targeting and then pull them up in the SERPs.

For example, ABC Consults is a corporate law firm in Victoria Island Lagos, Nigeria. In the site identity description, it would make sense to say: "ABC Consults, corporate law firm in Victoria Island Lagos" or something similar so that search engines will take note of this and make sure that you rank for your locality in the SERPs.

So, it is important to not only target keywords, think of targeting local keywords that are relevant to your areas of specialization so that your law firm's website can attract qualified leads and prospects.

Include your business name, local address, and all contact details on prominent locations on the website so that site visitors can easily contact your law firm with their queries.

Conclusion

It all boils down to the effort you make over time. The little efforts matter. You may think that the list of things you need to do for your law firm website is too long, but you can tackle these per post, per page, per directory, per high quality external link. The little efforts will build up over time to a cohesive output that will help your law firm get branded and noticed online.

Chapter Five

Using LinkedIn to Market your Law Firm or Law Practice

INTRODUCTION

LinkedIn is the top social media platform for professionals. From doctors, to lawyers, to social media marketers, everyone is getting on the LinkedIn platform and trying to use it to grow their careers and advance their company profiles. LinkedIn is to professionals what Facebook is to a Gen Z young man or woman. It has risen to become one of the fastest growing social networks in the world, with hundreds of thousands of professionals and companies using the platform daily.

LinkedIn is an extraordinarily potent platform, even more so than Facebook. Please note that we are not interested in denigrating Facebook in any way—the platform is a massive social media platform for individuals and Brands. However, for law firm discourse, it is irrelevant to this discourse and we are focusing almost exclusively on the B2B platform, LinkedIn. The reason is simple. LinkedIn is a network that connects *only* professionals across varying fields from all over the world. While Facebook has room for only 5,000 connections, LinkedIn has room for 30,000 personal connections, plus (room for) countless millions of followers if a user can swing it. In order to be able to swing it, however, far more time and effort is needed than on Facebook.

What makes LinkedIn different, you ask? What makes it different is that LinkedIn carters to professionals and businesses, both B2B and B2C. Thousands of professionals sign up on the platform every year, and more are being added on the daily. Furthermore, thousands of companies use LinkedIn to advance their company profiles and gain top of mind awareness from leading professionals across the Globe.

As a lawyer—and it is immaterial whether you are a young lawyer who's still fresh out of Law School or a lawyer with fifteen years PQE—having a social presence on LinkedIn makes more than enough sense for your career. Not only that, it is helpful to establish a professional footprint for you online if and when people search for you.

Please note: LinkedIn is vast, with users spanning across the entire length and breadth of the whole world. And what's more, you have the ability to connect with thousands of like-minded individuals if and when you start leveraging the power of LinkedIn for your social legal marketing.

> "LinkedIn is Branding and Marketing on Steroids."

On LinkedIn, the power to sell without really selling takes a new meaning. Thousands of professionals use the platform, many to advertise, some to be passive participants who merely observe the platform, and yet others with the drive to further develop their personal brands and push their company profiles out to potential clients and customers.

How Can LinkedIn be Useful for Your Law Firm?

LinkedIn is the world's largest professional network that connects millions of professionals around the world together. Another feature that makes LinkedIn great is the fact that there is room for companies to create their company profiles on the platform so that they have a presence, post their updates, and also link back to their website (if you have one, and you should).

According to Forbes, LinkedIn drives 64% of all social media visits to a company website. Furthermore, people use LinkedIn to research the companies and Firms they're interested in, and your potential clients will use the Platform to research you and your law firm when the time is right.

You have effectively set up the website for your law firm, now it's time to set up your law firm's LinkedIn profile. These all adds up in your legal marketing efforts. Creating a profile requires more than just creating a profile; it requires putting in the effort to get viewers on to that company profile for them through the publication of articles, sharing tips, and generally keeping the profile alive and worth visiting over time by prospects.

Law Firms That Use LinkedIn

The world has its great law firms: those ones that have thousands of employees across hundreds of offices in different jurisdictional seats, focusing on servicing clients across diverse practice areas around the Globe. These law firms have company LinkedIn profiles for their law firms, with thousands of followers following their pages so as to receive updates and newsletters when they publish them.

For law firms with massive followership on the platform, they have the capacity to reach more people with their value proposition. They have the capacity to reach thousands of prospects through their organic reach and even through targeted advertising on the platform. They can reach literally thousands of people with their marketing materials and practice area offerings (if they have such a wide reach). Even for the law firms with profiles which are not flooded with followers, marketing is still possible through the use of hash tags and the creation of paid marketing campaigns on the firm's LinkedIn company profile.

Top Tips on Using LinkedIn to Market your Law Practice/Firm

The advice included below will encompass both solo practitioners and law firm teams who're seeking to create a unified presence on the world's largest professional network.

Build a Great LinkedIn Profile:

A simple LinkedIn search will show those that come up for the different search terms you type into your search bar. Depending on your search parameters, you can search for people in a particular field, geographical location, interests and so on. You can search people by exact job descriptions. You can search for people based on the Universities they attended. You can even search for people based on keywords that you want to receive search results for.

Thus, it is important for you to build a very killer profile. After you go through the LinkedIn login, you fill *ALL* the boxes when filling your LinkedIn profile details. I personally think it is vitally important to leave nothing blank. Here's what can help you:

- ➤ Your LinkedIn headline should be filled to reflect your core beliefs and chosen profession. It can also showcase a short summary of what you do for people. It should focus on your professional life; I mean, the aim of registering on the platform is to leverage it for business, am I correct?

- ➤ Your LinkedIn profile summary should be captivating and capture your professional essence. Write this preferably using the first person narrative and make sure that this summary captures your professional path. It could also showcase how you add value to other professionals. Have fun writing this, but be truthful and ensure that you cut off all fluff from the narrative.

- ➤ Upload Slideshare presentations and other media that can showcase what you do or what you have done in the past for your legal clients. They may be pictures of you and your team attending bar conferences, pictures or slides of you making a seminar presentation or keynoting a speech. If you think there is a media you have in your archives that have professional relevance, you can use it. These all add up in building your narrative. Be spare about it, though.

- ➤ Write to professionals who have worked with you in the past and ask for recommendations. Many will be glad to write recommendations for you if they feel that you are worth it. You can ask your former law firm bosses, partners, and even clients to write recommendations for your profile. This will serve as a profile booster as many professionals [myself included] will not write a recommendation for a fellow professional unless they are absolutely sure of the professional reputation of the person they're writing the recommendation for.

If you are in charge of your law firm marketing, then check through and see if the members of your team have professional profiles on LinkedIn. If they do, look for the best ways to optimize the look and feel of their profiles. Take a deep scrutiny of their entire profiles, from professional headshot to their publications. If they don't have LinkedIn profiles, you know what to do: have them get on the network and connect with each other. They should also give endorsements and ask for endorsements from connections and others in their network. And more importantly, they should engage, engage again and further engage with the users of the platform. Being dormant renders the exercise a useless one, can we agree on that?

Creating Content: Consistently Provide High-Quality Content

There are thousands of professionals on LinkedIn. However, the ones that become the stars of LinkedIn are those that consistently provide value. By providing high-quality content for the other professionals on the platform, you showcase your thought leadership; you display your thought processes and also showcase your take on Industry-related issues. You can also use the platform to showcase your personality.

By training, lawyers are trained to be critical, analytical, solve problems, and to write. Lawyers do all these extensively because of the briefs they handle for clients consistently. There is no better place to showcase those critical reasoning skills and writing prowess than on a professional platform like LinkedIn.

Your content can take the form of simple posts. LinkedIn restricts their simple posts character count, so a LinkedIn writer doesn't have much space to play around with. However, it will make you learn to maximize your minimal space and use it well to capture exactly the essence of what you want to capture for your reading audience. It will make you to utilize the given word count you can play with very well so that you push past your post's character count; LinkedIn won't let you do that.

Articles: You can take to writing articles for your LinkedIn audience. With LinkedIn articles, you have more space to play around with. On the plus side, the articles written and published on LinkedIn Publisher are permanent in nature and also rank in search engines if the keywords are searched for.

One strategy that can help you to create content consistently for LinkedIn is to create a content calendar. Your content type can be split into thought leadership posts [that will help you showcase your industry knowledge in your field of operation] and other content types. You can also harness the power of LinkedIn video to reach your audience and reach hash tags to maximize exposure to prospective readers who are interested in the topics you write on.

LinkedIn Video Tips:

LinkedIn Video is a relatively new roll-out on the platform. Because of that, LinkedIn is trying to push its video feature out to its users so they can adopt its use. That makes videos on the platform popular and capable of reaching large audiences.

Top Tips: Find your own voice. Be unique. Some people are bogged down with other people's ideas of how to write or not to write on LinkedIn. What we can tell you is to find your own unique voice when writing for LinkedIn. Just look for a way to pass your message across to your audience and you will be fine. Some lawyers have had course to write using Nigeria's pidgin English; some write using a mixture of English and other languages—what matters most is that you pass your message across to your readers and they understand you.

Network

Networking is extremely important for professionals, particularly among young professionals who are seeking to gain footholds in their chosen careers. A professional network of people either in the same exact profession or those in sister professions can help your career growth.

"Your network is your net worth."

Harnessing your professional network is extremely vital, and what better way to seek your network out than through LinkedIn?

Networking in this sense goes beyond sending and accepting connection requests. It goes beyond liking and commenting on other professionals' posts on LinkedIn [though these help, anyhow, as it helps you gain visibility within your network]. Within this context, Networking means reaching out actively to your connections; sharing interesting posts, calling these networks if and when the occasion calls for it, and keeping actively in touch with them. Are they working within the same area you are? Meet up for drinks or coffee or lunch. Are they looking for jobs and you "happen" to know a job that may be a good fit for their unique skill sets? If you know that they are a good fit, why not refer them? Are you attending a conference which other members of your professional network is attending? Great, send them a message to see if you can meet up at intervals.

No other network helps like-minded professionals to come together than LinkedIn; use this to your advantage. It can open some doors which you don't expect.

Reach out to old colleagues and old classmates of yours. Join LinkedIn Groups of your choice and contribute actively to the conversations there. Sadly though, LinkedIn hasn't maximized the use of Groups, which means that some groups with thousands of members don't receive the kind of attention such a group would ordinarily receive if it were on Facebook.

Your Law Firm Profile

By creating a law firm profile on LinkedIn, the firm's profile can come up on search engines when someone searches for it on search engines. The law firm also has areas where they can create the summary of the profile, add number of members working in the firm, the firm's telephone numbers and contact email address, and the firm website. On the plus side, LinkedIn matches the profile of the firm's team mates on the platform to that law firm profile so that viewers can click to view the entire employees (including past attorneys who have moved on to other roles in other organizations) of the firm who have profiles on LinkedIn.

It is imperative that the LinkedIn profile searchers see for your law firm reflects your true values as an organization and portrays your people in good light.

Chapter Six

Use of Content Aggregators and Article Directories

INTRODUCTION

It is inarguable that Content is the bane of the Internet. Every website hosted on the Internet is populated with all types of content, including written and visual content. Some websites have more content than others and have more search engine visibility than others. Some websites are structured as article directories and have their own built-in subscriber base that follows the articles published on those websites.

The way to marketing is through content. Content is a function of marketing. Marketing has evolved over time, and content that geared towards advertising have also changed and evolved over time. Place ads on websites and readers that visit that website either click out of the website or they ignore the ads entirely. Run ads on TV programs and viewers will make use of the remote control to change to another channel so they don't have to view your obtrusive advertisement.

The truth is that people do not like the conventional, traditional advertising model of the past anymore. People have so much to distract them, they now make and the use the most opportunities to reduce the number of distractions around them. We have all agreed that direct advertisements is a distraction many people would rather do without.

Why Should My Law Firm Use Content Aggregators?

These are platforms that pull together content focusing on specific niches to their audience who have specific interest in that subject matter. The advantage of this is that they already have a built-in audience for their content rather having to source for readers across the far-flung corners of the World Wide Web.

Mr. A, a corporate attorney, may be interested in keeping abreast with the happenings in the corporate world around the Globe. He'd perhaps look for the best content aggregator that delivers the type of content he needs, subscribes to it, and gains access to myriad content from different publishing houses (Firms).

Thus, the same approach Mr. A the corporate attorney will take will be the same approach another person will take, and so on. So, there will be a massive readership already developed in the area a law firm is trying to get visibility for in these websites, so keying into them would make sense, wouldn't it?

Choosing the Best Platform for your Legal Content

A strategy will be instructive, in this regard. For example, an attorney or law firm servicing clients in Nigeria would be better off using Lexology than using JD Supra as their content aggregator of choice to deliver their content to their target audience. The former aggregator has thousands of users from Nigeria who are subscribed to read the insights published by contributor firms and writers on the platform which are delivered either daily or weekly to the email addresses of their subscribers. Lexology would deliver these insights to their subscribers according to the preferences of these subscribers by jurisdiction, practise areas and trends.

JD Supra would probably be a bad idea for a law firm or lawyer in Nigeria to publish on because they carter to a predominantly American audience. Lexology carters to American audiences too, but at least Nigerian users use Lexology more than they would use JD Supra.

So, studying the trends and user base, alongside the reach of these aggregators, would help you determine which one to go with.

Setting a Budget

Going this route definitely requires a yearly marketing budget. The reason is simple: these platforms have made the consistent effort over the years to develop their subscriber base which will probably consist of other lawyers (who will be a great referral source or collaborators on practise areas they cannot handle if they deem your firm to be a subject matter expertise in that area of Law), corporate in-house counsel, and sophisticated professionals from other fields. What this means is that your firm's marketing team is trying to buy into a solid user base, and it's not free. It is *never* free. It is part of paid Media, and law firms with the budget and earnings to cover these costs usually use these aggregators.

Contact the sales team of Lexology or Mondaq or JD Supra or whichever service you would like to use for your law firm marketing and find out the costs associated with being a contributor firm to their publication list. Past research revealed that the billing is annual; you have to then find out what the exact price is. Can your firm handle it? Can they pay for it? Does your law firm have enough catchy content on its website to decide to publish with these platforms? (Read back on the chapter that talks about using content in your law firm marketing effort) Do you think the extra pair of international Eyes on your law firm's thought leadership content is worth paying for?

This is something the law firm's marketing team may want to discuss with senior Management to see if it is a good fit. They might also want to find out precise subscriber and engagement figures from the user demographic your law firm is trying to target with its content. That way, you can make a good prediction of who your content will be visible to if you decide to use the content platform of your choice. Then you can dive in.

However, please note that it is not about setting up profiles with these legal article directories and submitting articles through your Firm profile. The type of content submitted matters. For each subscriber, scores of articles based on their user preferences with regards to legal subject matter and jurisdiction are usually sent to them and they have to make their choice as to which of the articles to read. High-quality articles aimed at educating your target audience will yield more dividends than bland articles loaded with legalese. Legalese is good, of course, but only if it's a lawyer reading it. A non-lawyer reading through loads of legalese will be undoubtedly put off and click away from the article. There's no doubt about that. Most people complain that the legal profession is loaded with obscure, esoteric terms and near-incomprehensible arguments; using the same technique lay people complain about is not going to yield any dividends. It could end up being a waste of your law firm's marketing dollars.

Measuring ROI and other Metrics

There is no doubt that the use of content aggregators and platforms can be expensive. It can eat into a law firm's marketing budget for them to take out subscriptions and market to the subscriber base on the platforms through the subtle art of selling without selling. Larger law firms may have the annual budget that can fund these ventures whereas the mid-tier to smaller law firms may have issues around budgeting.

It is important and vital for whoever is in charge of the content marketing of the law firm to ensure that they measure the metrics for their efforts. Visibility, engagement, and click-backs into the law firm's website and static landing pages are important. By measuring the performance of your ad spend—for these qualify as ads in my opinion—you learn what works and what doesn't work for your law firm in its marketing efforts.

Chapter Seven

Adapting Specific Strategies

INTRODUCTION

The mistake a lot of attorneys make is that they do not know how to sell to their target audience. Many lawyers think like lawyers when they approach their prospects (or rather, the other way round). In many cases, this leads to the loss of the prospect. Afterwards the attorney may be left wondering what went wrong and why he couldn't close the prospect. Some lawyers close these prospects and the lifetime value of that (now paying) client may be worth a lot in legal work and yearly revenue.

Story for Illustration

Adrian is a business lawyer with his offices in the central business district of Lagos Island. He attends a once-a-month breakfast meeting at Eko Hotel in Victoria Island. Seated beside him is a distinguished-looking man who introduces himself as Anthony Obi, the founder of a small company operating there in the Island. Adrian is pleased and hopes to strike up a meaningful conversation that can lead to this Anthony becoming either a potential client or a referral source for his law practise. He launches into a long conversation with Anthony; he explains the business clientele he's serviced across Lagos. He talks about his practise and the other man talks about his business. At the end of the meeting, Anthony walks away.

Adrian doesn't think he's closed this man effectively. He ponders what happened there at the business meeting.

Analysis

What he doesn't know is that he acted precisely like a lawyer, knowing only how to push his practise in the best way he knows how and nothing more. He did not go further; he did not dig into the man's psyche. In order to stand a chance of landing Anthony, the best thing he could have done was to think like Anthony; he ought to put himself in Anthony's shoes as a business owner/manager. What legal issues could Anthony be facing in the business? What compliance issues is he either aware of but doesn't know how to handle or is completely unaware of? What legal issues is he likely to come up against in the line of business his company is engaged in? How would a lawyer help Anthony out?

If Adrian was able to mentally ruminate on these and came up with practical legal solutions in his head, the relationship could have been deepened from there. Furthermore, if he had industry specific knowledge of the sector Anthony is servicing, he could have become a better source of information to the man and that could have deepened their relationship.

> *In order to be able to make an impact on them, you have to be like them. You have to understand them and what makes them tick.*
>
> **Anonymous saying.**

Localizing Your Strategies

The marketing strategy that would work for a boutique New York commercial litigation law firm would be unlikely to work for a Lagos commercial litigation law firm. While New York and Lagos are both metropolitan cities, with sizable chunks of sophisticated business men and women, the demography and culture are completely different. Plus, New York would qualify as a mature services market whereas Lagos wouldn't—the latter is a developing Market.

Plotting and replicating the strategy utilized by a global Firm like Baker & McKenzie will probably flop horribly if done for a small firm that services only a particular segment of corporate clients in Abuja, Nigeria.

Law firm marketing success will depend on an offering that puts the target clients' cultural and geographical identities into deep consideration. For example, a law firm in Onitsha Nigeria will have to adopt a marketing strategy that is completely different from the strategy plotted for a law firm in Victoria Island, Lagos even if it's the same marketing strategist that plotted the strategy playbook of both Firms. Why? This is because of the vital need for Ultra localization of marketing strategies, since what works for a law Firm in one location will *not* work for another law Firm in a different location, or servicing a different category of clients.

In order to achieve a laser-focused localization of strategy, research, analysis, understanding of the target market and the type of law practise that can thrive in that target geographical market, are all important factors that will determine if your strategy is going to work or if it is going to flop. In other words, you have to conduct your **SWOT** analysis.

You have to evaluate your strengths, find your weaknesses, identify the opportunities open to you, and check out the threats that may serve as stumbling blocks to your law practise. Let us illustrate below.

SWOT Analysis

This is the **Strength, Weakness, Opportunity, and Threat** Analysis that has been undergone to map out the core factors that will influence the start-up of the law firm, if it is a law firm that has yet to begin operations. For an already operational entity, its aim would be to identify core considerations for the firm.

> **Strengths**

What is the strengths of this law firm? What does it have that can give it an edge over other law firms practicing within the same locality? A law firm that is Digital focused may have the strength of the firm hinged on the fact that it has its vision and eyes set to the forefront of the current digital trend that is disrupting the entire corporate world and taking everyone by storm. If other law firms within the locality practice "conventional" law, then they have a unique edge which they can leverage in their operations.

> **Weakness**

What is the firm's weakest link? What are the advantages other firms have over your own law firm? For example:

The weakness of the firm could be that the firm is a relatively new firm, and at such, is unknown. Also, the issue of startup finances will pose a severe problem since a lot is needed in order to put the firm to ground. This might affect the initial client base the firm will have in the immediate future.

The above could be a weakness, and the law firm should be ready to tackle it from the roots.

> **Opportunities**

Are there business opportunities in the target Market that your law firm can leverage to grow? If yes, then what are these opportunities it can key into? It could be that the firm has a lot of opportunities to key its practice into the booming corporate and Business stratospheres which the big-playing law firms that dominated the legal services marketplace in that locality had long keyed into in booming practice areas of the law.

Identifying potential opportunities and sources of new business for your law firm is germane to its growth trajectory.

> **Threats**

What are the factors that can affect your law firm growth, visibility and relevance in its target marketplace? For a new law firm that just appeared recently on the horizon, the Threats consideration could be: the monopoly of the lucrative, high-paying corporate clients by the Big Law; harsh economic realities that threaten the provision of legal services since companies are downsizing their budget due to bleak economic forecasts.

The Localization Process

Localization of your law firm marketing strategy is going to be a complex process that will take into account, a lot of questions and considerations that may take time to articulate. A cultural and impact analysis needs to be conducted and comprehensively set down in a report that will be pored over with the aim of drawing up the very best strategy that is going to work for your target market. Your marketing specialists' localization analysis and research needs to consider the following:

1. The people who live and work in the target geography: are they educated or people with little to no formal education?

2. If they are educated, do they work in the corporate world or they do they have their own boutique consulting practice? If they are not educated, what precisely do they do for a living? What type of businesses do they operate?

3. Consumer trends, preferences, and preferred means of communication.

4. Cultural norms of your target market.

5. The behaviour of the people in the target market towards professional services providers. Are they types that understand that they need professionals in various facets of life? Or are they those that believe they have *no* need *whatsoever* for professionals? Or more specifically, that they have no need for lawyers?

This research is important not only for your digital marketing and advertising; it encompasses the entire considerations your marketing department needs to look at before coming up with location address, slogans, brand imagery and outlook, operational style and then the actual functioning of your law firm brand to service its desired clientele. If you understand that law practise in one of the locations your law firm is trying to service is largely focused on civil litigation, real estate management and criminal litigation, it wouldn't make sense to start devising strategies to set up a mergers & acquisitions practise group there. One of your other branches can take that up, but remember, it has to absolutely fit, or the effort would be largely useless. If the locality is notorious for being highly litigious, which means that high volumes of litigation go on there over and above any other type of law practise, it would make no sense to develop an intellectual property practice group within that location.

Localization of your law firm's strategies requires noting down several key considerations and working in line to ensure that those considerations are handled so that they do not obstruct the growth of the law firm down the line.

Chapter Eight

Advice

Advice for Lawyers

Every lawyer is a professional, and in spite of what the century has turned into, lawyers remain some of the most highly respected professionals in the professional services world. So it goes to tell you pretty much that lawyers are very much respected.

Because of this respect people have for their Brothers in the long robes, it affects the way they interact with lawyers. Some lawyers are able to bank on that inherent respect while some others cannot. For those who cannot, please note this quote: Every attorney out there has to learn to sell themselves.

Confidence is the best outfit a lawyer can ever put on.

Wise saying.

Lawyers have a lot going for them. Their technical field of study has set them apart from the other courses in the Arts. Lawyers were revered in the past; they were seen from a high pedestal which many people aspired to have their children and wards attain. Times may have changed, but every lawyer is advised to remember the respect lawyers generally garner in the society.

Story Point

If a trader has a large store, then he can easily hire people to work for him and leave the business to travel. If something happens to him, the business moves on. If an attorney is a sole practitioner with his own practise, and something happens to him, then all hell will break loose. He has learned to rely on something: his brain. It's the bane of his profession. Without his thinking and analytical skills, he has nothing going for him. Any debilitating life event that happens to him will come with massive consequences for his finances. Without the technical knowledge he's amassed over the years, he has nothing. That means that he has to keep working in order to keep earning over the years.

A trader can have a highly sought-after product in the market and people will always seek out that product because they need it and because the trader stocks it. Conversely, a lawyer's work is services-based. Never forget that. The work a lawyer does for his clients is based on relationships he has with the client and how he can sustain it while at the same time solving the problems of his clients. If the client does not have business problems, then there will be no client-attorney relationship nor the provision of legal services.

A lawyer would do well to remember that it is easier to sell to a satisfied client over and over again, over the long passage of the years, and if possibly until the death of both parties, than it is to sell to a new client. So, it takes a great lawyer to maintain his good will with an old, satisfied client than to build a relationship with a new client.

Referral Sources

Lawyers understand better than those working in other professions that everyone they meet is a likely referral source for their legal services. The cleaner who works in the office may have a nephew who has a friend who resides in London and wants to invest $30,000.00 USD in the Nigerian real estate market. The sales girl you purchase goodies from the supermarket may have a young suitor who wants to purchase a new real estate property in a choice area of Lagos and need an attorney for the transaction because he knows no one to turn to for such a transaction.

Why make the above points about referrals, and how does that translate to legal marketing for law firms and attorneys?

Like I earlier pointed out, legal services providers maintain a relationship with their clients. It's a relationship business. Treat those that come your way well enough and you will potentially have great referral sources that can bring business your way. What's the essence of having clients who cannot refer their friends and associates to you when the latter category needs legal help? Furthermore, what is the essence of having clients that will not be interested in bringing their friends and family to your law firm if they need legal representation?

So, while many lawyers may want to overlook referrals as a legal marketing technique, it is important to note that client referrals remains one of the important ways a lawyer can generate new business from clients who were referred by the lawyer's satisfied clients.

Advice for Law Firms

Many law firms think that legal marketing is the exclusive work of a law firm's marketing department. They exclude their lawyers from their legal marketing efforts because they do not think that their attorneys have the experience or the know-how to market themselves and their firm's practise to the potential clients they meet out there. They leave the lawyers to their work and the lawyers leave the marketing department to their work; for those that have a marketing department.

Should this be so? Is that the best practice?

Remember previous paragraphs, or at least the part we mentioned the importance of seeing law as a relationship business? Well great, that applies here. People make their hiring decisions based on the individual members of a law firm; they do not hire because of the pedigree of the law firm. In some cases—particularly with institutional or corporate clients—they may see the law firm while overlooking the individual attorneys because they want to use the backing of Powerful law firms for their complex commercial transactions. That is where the power of the tier 1 and tier 2 law firms come in, where prospective clients come to those firms because of the *Name* of the law firms and the heft of the law firm's brand.

On the flip side, People see the attorneys; they do *not* see the firm. What they know is Mr. XYZ who is a great tax practitioner that worked with Ernst & Young for three years before entering a formal law firm environment. What Mr. B knows is that lawyer ABC is one of the greatest legal minds that can wade through the murky waters of election petition matters. What Mr. C knows is that lawyer B is a fantastic startup advisory lawyer with deep industry knowledge of the tech industry, so would make the ideal legal advisor for his latest tech company. They want to hire specific lawyers who may, in turn, constitute a team of legal Talent that will help them actualize the client's goals. The bigger fry see the law firm while the smaller fry see the practitioners in the law firm.

We know that lawyers are extremely busy professionals, in many cases overworked with the massive workload of their myriads of legal cases. Thus, they stay away from business development and brand marketing for their firms, because that is not their area and they do not have the patience and insight to add anything else to their workloads. Plus, there is something to be said about lawyers being bad in business—the proponents of this view may be right or they may be wrong—that's not the point. The point is that many lawyers do not see their legal services within the purview of business that helps them to pay the bills.

The point is that law firms should try as much as possible to be all-encompassing in their strategy; they should try to devise an inclusive strategy that will involve the input of their attorneys since it's the work of the entire attorneys in a law firm that makes them all fee earners. It is the combined work of the lawyers in the law firm that makes the law firm an entity. If the lawyers are not performing, then the law firm will, by extension, be deficient. A team is as strong as its weakest link, and the same is applicable to law firm environments.

We have seen situations where junior attorneys in a law firm are completely excluded from the firm's business development efforts; all they are ever allowed to do is to work based on the available briefs the "rainmakers" bring in. And in many cases, these "rainmakers" are the sole proprietor who owns the firm and has these other lawyers as employees working for him. Some attorneys complain that they don't get to see and interact with clients. Some are not aware of what the firm is doing to bring in new work, which will automatically translate to more work and more pay for everyone. Some are kept out in the dark when important decisions are being made. Some receive lesser pay than their fellow attorneys with the same post qualification experience based on office politics.

Case Study 1

ABC law firm is a ten-attorney firm with three support staff. The firm is structured as a sole proprietorship. The other attorneys in the firm who work for their employer do not know about their employer's business development efforts. They see clients only if and when necessary for them to interact with clients. They do not understand what it means to try and market their firm practise. They do not know if the employer is actively expanding the firm's contacts to see if more work could come in their way. Only one of the attorneys have an active LinkedIn account with ten thousand connections and counting. The firm has a website but they don't know whether they get prospects to the site or whether the firm closes some prospects through its website because their website work is outsourced to a web design & management agency in another city even though one of the junior attorneys is a computer guru and can manage the firm's website more than an outside firm ever can. Or at the very least, he can contribute towards making the firm's website one of the best within the physical location area of the law firm.

Everything around the firm is structured by and around the Proprietor. There is no room for dissent or the pollination of ideas from the other lawyers.

Analysis

The scenario we painted above points unwaveringly to the fact that the firm's lead attorney keeps a tight leash on things. It means there is no trust. Many attorneys complain of the lack of trust that exists in many law firms. There is inherent, deep-seated distrust across the entire hierarchy of the law firms.

Law firms ordinarily should be some of the easiest and most friendly places to work because of the highly technical nature of attorneys' work for clients. It should be places where Deep thinking takes place and ideas for thrown back and forth between fee earners. Do not get the wrong picture—in many law firms, these are obtainable. However, in a large number of law firms, the reverse is the case.

Business development efforts is not the work of the lead attorney, neither is it the work of the law firm partners. Business development entails a collective effort on the part of the fee earners, from the most senior to the most junior. It is the job of the lead attorney and the more senior lawyers to sharpen their business development skills, develop and hone a great focused strategy on how to maximize revenue for their law firm, then pass on the knowledge garnered to the more junior attorneys through coaching and mentoring as the Juniors transit from smaller roles to higher workloads and corresponding better pay for their work. Obviously, a junior attorney will not be a junior attorney forever; with the passage of the years, a junior attorney grows in experience and exposure. It wouldn't make sense for them to remain ignorant about business development and what the secret sauce is for them to be able to become "rainmakers" either if they later set up their own firm or if they make partner in their current firm.

Juniors need to be equipped with the skills that they need to succeed in the future, and that includes business development skills that will help them become rainmakers in the future.

With the above scenario painted, this much is obvious: the attorneys who are in firms where they cannot grow all round in legal expertise and business development acumen will definitely lack active business development skills, unless they specifically and individually make active efforts to update their business development knowledge, learn to plot strategy and implement same.

Case Study 2

DEF law firm is a ten-attorney firm with three support staff. The firm is structured as a loose partnership, with an official hierarchy of roles but an unofficial conglomeration of efforts across board. All the attorneys that work in the firm play an active part in the firm's business development efforts. They get to meet with the clients they work with. The younger attorneys attend client meetings with the partners and actively shadow them in the work the partners do. The members of the firm hold monthly retreats and actively plot strategies about how to further grow the firm's practice.

Everyone is trained to learn to market their firm practise in everything they do. The firm has an external strategist who is the founder of a top legal marketing agency.

All the attorneys have an active LinkedIn account with ten thousand connections each at the minimum. The firm has a website that is managed by an external agency but under the project supervision of one of the firm's attorneys who was a content writer for international publications for some years before becoming an attorney. The same attorney is the law firm's content marketing strategist and draws up the firm's content marketing calendar so that each attorney can contribute their thought leadership to it based on their own individual areas of practise.

All the firm's attorneys actively promote the law firm's content across various social media channels. They individually strive to get featured in business publications. They speak at conferences. One of the junior attorneys hosts an interactive webinar once every two months to discuss issues of law. All the attorneys have profiles on top legal directories. They all strive to build up the firm's image while also building and marketing their individual brands.

Question

Between firm ABC and firm DEF, which do you think will have more visibility across the country, get eyes on their website, and have more prospects checking them out to see if they can utilize the firm's practise expertise for their legal issues?

Your guess is as good as mine: firm DEF is the one with the goods and they are the ones that will come up in search engines; they are the ones with the visibility needed to reach their potential clients. They are the Firm whose attorneys are active rainmakers, all connected to the firm's success.

Key Takeaway

Law firm Marketing is *not* an activity that can kept under wraps between key contacts in a firm. What if something happens to those key contacts? Say, a debilitating illness, or, worse still, death. What happens? Who can, or what can, sustain the firm they left behind since the attorneys there understand little to nothing about how the law firm really works?

We have seen law firms crumble into extinction with the death of the lead attorney. Several of them still have the shingles of the name of the law offices hung out to the view of the public, crumbling testimonies of a past now forgotten because it couldn't be sustained. With the death of the owner of the law firm, clients come to carry their litigation files to go for another firm; junior attorneys scamper off and head to other law firms or go to take in the gauntlet and set up their own small law firms. Several years of work on a "Name"; a Brand, gone as if it never existed.

So, from the start, it is very important for law firms to define a cohesive strategy for their marketing efforts and how they can ensure that their attorneys are a part of this strategy. After all, the Firm *is* the lawyers and the lawyers *are* the firm. If they understand the inner workings of the firm, it makes it easier for them to do their job and really be a part of the firm. Granted, there is certain information that needs to be retained only among senior or management level partners and dispensed to the lower hierarchy of attorneys on need to know basis, but marketing and exposure to the firm shouldn't be a part of it. The attorneys should be involved in the firm's business development efforts.

Plotting an Exit Strategy: Define your Successor

The work in many law firms revolve around the firm lead attorney. Many do not allow other attorneys to have their hands in the operations of the law firm, neither do these other attorneys have a clue as to client intake mechanisms, the firm's overall billing strategy. In some cases, other attorneys do not have professional semi-autonomy to do their work without over-arching control from the lead attorney.

In instances such as these, if the lead attorney dies, or is in any way incapacitated such that he cannot function in his work, then the overall marketing of the firm suffers. The reason is simple: with the entire work, marketing, client intake and other efforts revolving around the lead attorney in a firm, it becomes difficult for the other members of the law firm to key into the core efforts of the firm. With the (possible) death or permanent disability of the lead attorney, the other attorneys in a firm may be stuck in a rut. Clients may come for their (litigation) files to move them to other law firms, many prospects may pivot into other law firms; even the firm attorneys may exit from the firm. That drains a Brand fast, leaving once-thriving Brands to become shadows of their past glories.

All these generally happen in instances where the lead attorney who originally set up the firm never envisaged the continuation of the law firm long after they are gone. They do not envisage having successors other than family members to take over the firm; but in many cases these family members have other priorities. It is an impossibility that someone's later generations must become lawyers so they can carry the law firm name forward for years, for as long as they can sustain it.

Defining a successor doesn't necessarily tie in with the death of permanent disability of the lead attorney who'd set up the law firm. Creating a successor is more of a mental exercise that allows the owner(s) of a law firm to answer several key questions:

> ➤ *If something happens to me, who can take over this law firm:* By taking this question into consideration, the attorney is forced to develop long-range thoughts about the long-term strategy and

survival of the law firm. That way, several measures can be put into place: excel sheets created with the names and contact details of the firm's clients; the entire work processes and key contacts of the Firm's operations documented for future reference and use. Sadly, in many cases, fee earners in law firms would want to make partner whereas the owner of the law firm would want to pass the firm on to his kids. Since these two intendments are opposites, it creates a problem. Seasoned attorneys leave the firm. The younger generation of the law firm owner may not be interested in running law firms and instead, have other plans for their lives.

➤ *If I want to leave the legal profession for a one-year sabbatical, can my firm remain functional:* Law is a gruelling profession that requires total and absolute focus. With the overriding and constant changes in the dynamics of the society, the laws are modified continuously to feed this dynamic, and every attorney is expected to aggressively keep abreast with these developments. In many cases, over time, this may become overwhelming and demand a change from the rigors of the profession, even if for a short while. In that instant, can the attorney leaving the firm he'd set up be assured that the firm can function at optimum performance in his absence? If yes, if the other attorneys are equipped with the knowledge of the firm's working model and there are processes and procedures for the Firm's work, then the lead attorneys can make their exit. If no, then a strategy needs to be devised so as to render the constant physical presence of the law firm founder unneeded.

Top law firms in New York, London, and several parts of the world have clearly defined succession strategies. Many law firms are currently setting up formal law firm succession strategies and rigorously planning partner succession in the event of retirement or death so as to be prepared for the transition process. Many leading commercial law firms have already successfully transited from the first generation owners of the law firms to another generation of fee earners and managers that will continue to operate the law firm and ensure that its operations do not die out.

Lack of Succession Planning in Law Firms

Many law firms are sole practitioner firms and sole proprietor firms. For the former, many of them have that structure because they are unable to scale due to lack of availability of the type of clientele that will help them scale. Or it could be that the owners are not interested in operating mammoth law firms with several lawyers practicing Law under a single Firm umbrella. For the latter, many of them maintain that structure because the founders of these firms want to retain control over everything and maintain a hold over the client count. The firms which have a sole proprietorship structure usually have a high turnover of lawyers because the lawyers working in such firms don't see room for long-term career growth in these firms and they end up leaving to either start up their own firms (which, in many cases, is usually the same sole proprietorship structure earlier mentioned) or join other firms where they may get semi autonomy. Some leave because they want some level of flexibility in their working schedule—and this applies also to even the larger law firms, if not more so.

However, there are some law firms that have defined partnership structure, and this is usually seen in the top commercial law firms where there are transition mechanisms in place.

Nigerian Law Firms are Not Designed for Differentiated Branding

Being Nigerians, it would be best if some scenarios are localized to our home country as it pertains to practicing Law within the jurisdiction. Sadly, many law firms in Nigeria have the naming style that usually goes thus: Okoro Chambers, Benson Ibeziako & Associates (Grace of God Chambers), Ani Chambers (Law Firm of K. B. Ani, S.A.N.), Ituma, Ituma & Associates (Legal Practitioners and Corporate Consultants). Please note that foreign law firms utilize this structure too, though the focus on Nigerian firms here is so as to point out certain defects in our law firm succession system within the country.

From the above, it becomes glaring that the branding of the law firm is irremovably tied to the names and personality of the founders of these law firms. Law firms in Lagos and Abuja usually try to different the branding of the partners from the overall Firm branding to make for long-term continuity, but elsewhere across the country, the situation is different.

Because of this lack of differentiated branding, if the founders of many Nigerian law firms dies or reaches retirement age, the firm either closes shop immediately or goes downhill from there because the "Name" associated with the law firm is no longer available to oversee the running of the law firm.

Planning Long Term Succession Strategy

Creating a Law firm succession strategy is not a strategy plan that can be done within a day or a week. It requires a long term effort on the part of law firm Management to identify potential key leaders in the team that has the potential capacity to lead the law firm over time. Or, even if there is a lot remaining to be done before identifying potential key leaders in law firms that will potentially take over management of the law firm in the future, it will make a lot of sense for law firms that have the intention of creating a transition from the first generation handlers to 2nd generation managers over time to develop streamlined processes for *everything* they handle.

The last part could be illustrated with a "thriving" law firm situate somewhere in Lagos. Everything seems to be working perfectly for the law firm in their Lagos offices. Mr. A is a client of the firm. He routinely visits the Lagos Island offices of the law firm in question to get advised on legal matters. He has noticed that every time he comes to the law firm, he has to see the principal attorney in the firm. Furthermore, he has noticed that this principal owner is always answering phone calls on his phone ceaselessly for different issues; he is always bombarded with calls from associates and external contacts calling in with different issues that need to be handled.

It seems like a very busy beehive of activity. Mr. A had recourse to come to the law firm when this principal travelled to London for the graduation ceremony of a son. It seemed as if the clients had fled. Decisions were ground to a halt. Associates seemed to have little to nothing to do on their hands. All of Mr. A's requests has to be routed through to the principal attorney in London before they can attend to him.

Sadly, this scenario—though fictional—may not be so far from the truth of what is obtained in many law firms. In cases like these, *everything* about the firm revolves around the owner, without whom anything meaningful can be done.

Choosing Firm leaders

It is not easy to start looking towards the distant future to touch on issues pertaining to the successors of the principals in law firms, but it is a necessary evil. It is something that should be kept in the back burner because you don't want to address certain issues.

Are you a law firm principal? Have you asked yourself whether your law firm will continue working perfectly like a well-oiled machine if you are not there or whether it will be plunged into lethargy? If the law firm is going to operate optimally if you are not there for a while, then congratulations, you are doing a good job of setting structures in place. If your law firm will be plunged into lethargic inactivity when you are not there for some time, then note that there is a serious issue that needs urgent consideration.

You have to start early to define and scrutinize the crop of lawyers working with/for you to know who the shoe will best fit amongst them in the event of your (prolonged) absence. Is there a book of business that a future leader can flip through to see the past and current clients of the law firm? Has the firm kept an email list of leads, prospects and clients they sell directly to through email marketing? Is there a unified Knowledge Base in the law firm systems that can be accessed if need be? Is there a Process Manual that details the processes to be taken in the event of the occurrence of any event or in the course of handling client files at the law firm?

If there isn't, then ask this very pertinent question: what will happen if the law firm principal becomes indisposed and cannot be in the thick of things anymore or if the law firm principal dies?

Succession Planning

Law firm succession planning entails the detailed monitoring of staff where they are measured in terms of productivity, drive, leadership qualities, alongside several other custom metrics that will help you determine those who are "Leader Material" amongst the crop of lawyers already working within the law firm. We are not insinuating that other lawyers do not know their work or are incompetent; we are merely pointing out that some people will be better suited for leadership roles than others who may be content to just follow strong leaders.

Furthermore, monitoring the client satisfaction rate with the lawyers can point to noticing those with great interpersonal skills. These skills will then—most probably—translate to having the people skills needed in a leader to make a difference in the operations of the law firm if and when the need arises.

Challenges

Because there is usually an inherent lack of trust in many lawyers and law firm owners, they will want the entire law firm operation to revolve around them. Sadly, many of them do not believe in "outsider" succession—which would mean being succeeded by people who are not blood family members. Principals in law firms usually want only their children to "inherit" their law firms. Because of that, they maintain an iron hold over the affairs of the law firm by refusing to identify younger lawyers with leadership potential to groom them for leadership roles. Even if there are potential leaders, these upcoming leaders become eased out when they feel these other lawyers are becoming bigger Names. In many cases, there is a knowledge deficit, because many lawyers tend to horde pertinent client information from associates because of the (irrational?) fear of the associates making away with their client lists and files. These breed a thriving atmosphere of distrust within law firms, thus effectively crippling long term planning.

Furthermore, many law firms in Nigeria do not know how to transition from one age of principals in the law firms to another age of principals. This leads the firms to "die" natural deaths with the death of the principals in these firms. Stemming from this, there is usually a scramble for files by associates; clients also come for their files if they perceive the principal of a law firm is either under the threat of retiring or has lost his life.

Sadly, this scenario is replicated in many law firms.

The Business of Law

Lawyers in Nigeria are not usually equipped to handle the business of law. Most are trained with the mindset that they need great analytical, problem-solving and legal skills that will enable them to handle their client deliverables with the utmost professionalism. Most of them are not tutored on the business side of the Law, wherein they learn the best client intake strategies, rainmaking qualities, the need to create innovative solutions for client problems, alongside the deep understanding that Law is like any other business and should be treated as such if they want to maximize the practice of Law.

The few that later patch on to the idea of Law as a business just like any other business are those that later actively work to modify their mindsets by understudying successful firms within their and outside their jurisdiction and undergoing training on how to maximize profitability for their law firms years down the line.

The above presents a huge lesson: any lawyer that wants to maximize profitability in their law firm practice should bear in mind that providing value for clients is tied to compensation for the value created. Furthermore, this value creation should be approached from a business-focused mindset. These can help propel growth.

Choosing a Law Firm Business Model: Which Route to Go?

Many attorneys set up their law firms because they (erstwhile associates in other existing law firms) don't want to continue working for their previous firms and earn little in the way of remuneration for their services. In some cases, the motivation is purely different: the would-be founders want to make their own name, using their own resources. In some cases, some want the autonomy and freedom in choosing their billable hours which they probably won't get in the course of working with an existing firm unless their bargaining power was so strong as to make them to be able to negotiate their terms of employment to suit their working times.

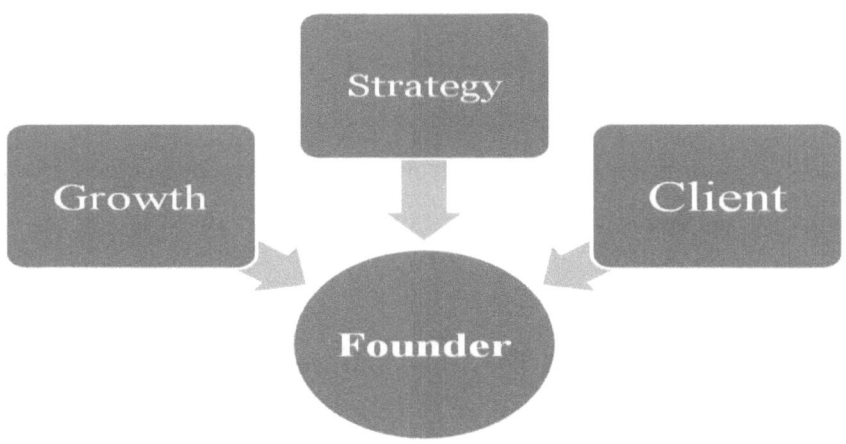

However, many founders of law firms consistently make the same mistake when setting up. They follow this trajectory:

1. Get office space

2. Hire support staff

3. Purchase office supplies

4. Hope for the best in the way of client intake and business boom

5. Rely on market forces to drive their Firm

However, in many cases, there is a serious problem with their adopted strategy as aforementioned (which is *no* strategy, by the way). Many lawyers rely on market forces for their client intake, retention and compensation. In this current disruption-based, innovation-moving economy, the legal services industry is a buyers' market, and relying merely on market forces to grow a new firm may prove to be disastrous.

Legal services consumers have become increasingly knowledgeable and sophisticated such that they understand the market and the underlying power they have. They also understand that now, rather than in the past when the model was relationship based, they have a big choice over which law firms to engage and which one to toss. They have precise ideas of what they want their legal services provider to do for their businesses and they expect their legal services provider to have the necessary resources, know-how and expertise to handle their work.

What Law Firms Founders Fail to Do

They Fail To Plan The Law Firm As a Business:

We discussed this issue briefly earlier in preceding sections. Law firms are like any other business. Many may argue that this is not the position, but it is worthy to note that professional services have been productized and have become profit-based because professionals are aggressively seeking to dominate their markets and retain a large chunk of their market share. That is why there is such expression as the "Business of Law". This translates loosely as the practise of law with the aim of making sizable profit for practitioners. Law firms must be strategically and seriously planned by the founders like the founders of companies seeking to have exponential growth. Several questions come into play, and each question must be comprehensively and surgically dissected and answered in order to gauge the level of preparedness of the founders of the firm seeking to have the firm on ground.

Questions like: who are we? What do we do? What are our core values? How do we work? What is our mission? What is our vision? What areas of law should we delve into? Who are our ideal clients for this firm? (in this case, such ideal clients should be comprehensively profiled, particularly as it pertains to age group and legal issues for which they may need the services of a law firm for) What are their demographics? Why would such already profiled clients choose the services of a new law firm over the services of already established law firms in the same location? Or why would they choose one law firm over the other? What are they factors they consider in making their legal buying decisions? What are the strengths the new law firm can boast of to use as a bargaining chip that will attract new clients? What areas of Law should the law firm streamline their practise to address for their clients? The questions are diverse and seemingly endless, but until the founders of a new firm are able to answer these seemingly innocuous but extremely important questions, then it means they might not be ready for the new leap. They may not be ready to truly begin operations. They may be relying on their emotions rather than hard facts and planning to set their Firm on the ground. They then rely on external factors to bring clients to their doorstep and they then have a practise that carters directly to the legal services needs of their clients. In this case, the clients are the ones streamlining and defining the law firm's practise for them.

Contrast the above with a law firm that streamlined its practise from inception, choosing to market their services to niche markets for niche practise areas. They have a working idea of who their ideal clients and they devise strategies to go about getting them. These practise areas will depend on the proficiency of the attorneys in them, as well as the deliberate choice to work within specific practise areas. Then the law firm practise expertise is marketed to the specific audience segment of their target market.

Here, in this latter case, the law firm exercises more control, rather than the client since they are not a do-all, be-all firm that works around their clients' needs. They have their specific service market and they operate within it to the clients that need those specific services which can range from complex M&A, Banking & Finance, Intellectual Property, Company post-incorporation matters, to commercial litigation, arbitration, or maritime Law. Or they could be providing services that cross the threshold of direct Law into multidisciplinary areas that require a more diverse range of skill sets than their conventional knowledge of the Law.

Growth Plan

Many law firms rely on luck to grow their business and develop to the heights they want it to develop to. This still boils down to thinking: founders and lead attorneys in law firms make the mistake of thinking that a law firm is not like any other business or company that needs strategic planning and business development ideas/plans to move ahead. They fail to ask questions pertaining to the best strategies they can follow to ensure that their firms are not left behind. In many cases, these attorneys do not know the type of questions to ask. However, if and where they don't, there are seasoned professional consultants that carter specifically to law firms, with a focusing of their consulting expertise on law firms.

Questions: How do we take over the market? How do we gain greater visibility? How do we become the top 1% out of the top 0.001% of the law firms practicing within the same city and across the same practice areas? What is the best management structure to utilize for the running of the firm? What is the employee structure? A partnership model? How do lawyers in the firm rise to partner level? Who controls equity in the firm profits? What will be the firm profit-sharing margins? How are studious, driven associates who bring in clients to the firm and who handles complex matters to stunning perfection be compensated? What about the need for outsourcing of issues like IT and law firm growth to specialists in their fields? How do we ensure our associates work within their areas of competence?

If a prospective founder can answer these questions, and if possibly, much more, then it may be a sure sign that the intended firm is on the right track. But if the founders of a firm are unable to answer these questions and more, then it may be a sure sign that they are not ready for the rigors associated with the Business of Law.

Institutionalization

It is a trend that many law firms fold up and close down with the death of the founding heads of the firm. Or in many cases, the old age of the founders. It could also be that they close down in the event of the incapacitation of the founder of the firm. If the founder of the firm becomes old or incapacitated, the firm loses its flavour and exits from the market. The firm folds up. Decades of established good will and client relationships gets washed down the drain. Within a short time, such firms are forgotten. It will then be as if they had never existed in the first place.

Creation of institutions is the key to long-term sustainable organic growth of a law firm. There should be a hefty, living strategy pertaining to how to institutionalize a firm and make the firm a self-servicing machine that will live on long after the demise of their founders. If and when done, then the good will of the firm, accumulated over decades of client servicing in the legal services sphere of the business world, will live on. The life and engine of the firm will continue to live on and service the firm for possibly countless decades after the death of the founders and heads of such firms.

Illustrations

Baker McKenzie: This law firm was founded in 1949 and currently ranked as the second-largest law firm in the world, with over 13,000 employees and over 4,000 fully employed revenue-earning lawyers in their employ, with at least 77 offices across 47 countries in the world. It is also ranked as the second largest law firm in the world in terms of generated revenue with US$2.67 billion in annual revenue earned in FY2017.

Headquartered in Chicago, USA, this firm is an international mega power in the legal services industry and services multinational corporations and top businesses across diverse corporate law practice areas.

A study of the exponential growth of this law firm from the time of its inception to the current times show that the firm did not arrive at its current destination by accident. It involved series of countless planning, strategic opening of offices across different cities in various legal climes: a joint venture satellite office was opened in Caracas, Venezuela, in 1955; from there, within the next three years, other offices were opened across Washington D.C., Amsterdam, Brussels, Zurich, New York. And from there, while imbibing a culture of growth, the firm expanded, and over the decades, has established itself as a major player in the world's international law practice.

It took more than market share and the number of their clients for them to keep expanding, setting up more offices in different jurisdictions, and hiring more and more fee-earners over time with the passage of the years.

Other Localized Illustrations

Olaniwun Ajayi LP: This is one of Nigeria's leading law firms with a strong team of lawyers across various practise areas. It is one of the country's leading commercial law firms and services a large slice of institutional clients across its three offices in Nigeria's leading commercial cities of Lagos, Abuja and Port Harcourt. Though this firm, likewise every other firm in the whole of Nigeria, will pale into insignificance in the face of the multi-continental law firms that rule law practice in the world, it is on its way to becoming a great self-powered institution.

The founder of the law firm, Sir Olaniwun Ajayi (of blessed memory, who died in November 2016) left a massive legacy for others to continue. Currently, the firm is pulling strong in the Nigerian legal sphere and has established itself as a reliable player in international legal circles, with several international deals under its belt. The firm was able to retain its standing as one of Nigeria's powerhouse law firms because of the dedication to long-term strategic growth and the implementation of great strategies.

The two firms listed above are merely small examples in a sea of countless many. There are top global behemoths that work to take over market share across various parts of the world, and, subject to jurisdictional regulations guiding law practise in these jurisdictions, they merge and expand over time. Some become reconstituted and subsumed under other thriving law firms with one goal in mind: expansion and growth.

The firms that managed to survive with the passage of the 1st generation founders are the firms that took growth, strategy, and long-term marketing very seriously. They are the firms that operate under iron-clad agreements, with thoroughly researched Plans set down in thick volumes for their lawyers to keep using as their playbook over the years. These playbooks are modified and edited with the passage of time and the changes in the legal atmosphere so that they can keep up and play better.

If and when the need arises, external consultants come in to help streamline the growth process to the needs of the Firm and the operations of the markets the firm operates in.

The Swiss Verein Model

Many law firms have several offices spread across various cities in high rises spread across the world. They have thousands of lawyers—many of whom become alumni as they either transit to consulting, open their own boutique firms, or move on to other roles in other leading law firms—who, between them, bill thousands of dollars' work in billable hours. They gather millions of dollars annually in profits.

Pick a large global law firm. The London offices of that law firm and the Chicago offices of the firm will exude the same ambience because the outlook and branding is fused. A visit to it Johannesburg offices will also showcase the same style similarities.

However, in the real sense of the word, these are not the same legal entity even though they bear the same name, utilize the same branding guidelines and imagery, and present a singular front to their global audience.

For years, mergers of larger multinational firms have followed the Swiss Verein model which allows strategy, branding, information technology and other functions to be shared between them. That way, a law firm operating in London with significant interests within Johannesburg can forward client work to the offices in Johannesburg. In this structure, clients are shared between partner firms as associated work spreads across multiple jurisdictions and faster local work is done if and when needed. Some work as referral partnerships, while others have a more centralized profit sharing pool. It depends on what the law firms adopting this structure want and whether the jurisdictions within which participating firms practice in allows such legal firm structures with outside Firms.

Several multinational law firms around the world have made this model work for them over the years. More are contemplating the Verein structure.

What is the Point?

The point is that law firms are adopting models which they feel will help them deepen their market share and global reach. They want to compete at a global level, and this structure seems to be the way to go for many of them, even though there may arise conflict of interest issues down the line. But we are not going there in this discourse because that is not the focal point we are reaching for.

The point is to point out the lengths highly competitive firms are willing to go to in order to further their objectives and deepen their market share. In the long run, you may not have the resources or reach to extend globally, but you have to keep making your moves to grow your practice and in turn, grow your annual revenue.

Bonus Sections

Becoming a Better Legal Marketer: It is your Duty

The wide view about lawyers is that they are professionals, not businessmen. They are and should be interested only in the professional side of their work. This can never be farther from the truth.

A person would go for a heart surgery at the hands of a surgical team who're highly trained in what they do. A product will gain market traction and penetration if it is something people have a demand for and if the marketing is done just right. The demand for this product doesn't necessarily have to be tied to the fact that people actively demand for it; in many cases consumers need a class of products without actually realizing that they need it. It is the duty of the products company to show the people that they need it.

The same is applicable to lawyers. Many lawyers enter the Bar with the thought and expectations that people "will come". They are professionals, after all, and people will seek them out if and when the need arises.

Relying on the above thought pattern would be a terrible mistake. The legal profession has eased out of conservative ways into competition, with profitability, gaining of market share, and long-term growth as the watchwords. For everything a lawyer is not doing to market himself, other lawyers are doing them and are even paying their way through the Media for them. You're not on LinkedIn? That colleague of yours you normally chat up at Bar meetings has fifteen thousand LinkedIn connections and is routinely invited as a speaker at conferences where he expands his network and markets himself to potential clients. Your law firm does not have a website? Great. The law firm on the tenth floor of the building across the street has a 5-year old law firm website with an SEO score of 45 and a monthly visitor count of around three thousand visitors, 0.9% of whom become clients or prospects closer in the sales funnel to closing. You rely on word-of-mouth? Sure, that's great. The law firm owned by your best friend has a management & innovation consultant on retainer, alongside a digital consulting firm on retainer to help them devise strategies through which they can expand their client base and gain market visibility.

Quote to Note:

"Lawyers have to learn to innovate or they die".

The death is figurative. If people do not know you or think you understand their problems enough to be able to proffer a solution, how then do you expect them to hire you? Chances are, they won't. People want to engage lawyers they perceive can solve their problems. Remember the keyword: perception.

A Scenario

Attorney A is a lawyer with three active years PQE and he has his own law practise. He has a website and has set up an online presence across different parts of the Web; his law firm website; his articles appears on trade magazines, digital publications and industry publications (some of which he's paid for). He's attended and spoken at several conferences. He writes in-depth legal articles through which he answers legal questions and educates readers on legal issues which he publishes and distributes to his newsletter subscribers three times a week. He has a defined work process and marketing strategy that he's been using to market his practise since he opened his doors to the public. He has an active email list of three thousand people he makes "outbound" marketing moves on.

Potential clients from his city always call his phone number and send in emails via the contact forms on his lead generation pages on his website. Many of them eventually convert into paying clients and he earns money from them.

The Analysis

This attorney has taken the time and the effort to market himself and his law practise. He does not have to rely only on the referrals clients bring his way. Referrals eventually do dry up, and what happens then? Being visible has been of immense benefit to him; prospects see his practise and news about him wherever they turn. Newspapers featuring him on their pages is proof of service of his expertise and understanding of clients' needs, at least in their own minds and perceptions.

In today's world, remember that professional services have become competitive. Marketing and strategic positioning remains key to gaining market share. As a lawyer—and it does not matter if you are working in a multi-national firm or engaging in solo practise—marketing yourself is essential. It is not all about developing thousands of connections on LinkedIn; really connecting with them and showcasing your legal expertise every chance you've got matters a lot in the long and short run. Being deliberate in your marketing efforts will definitely yield better dividends than staying put and waiting for referrals and clients to just come in and engage your services.

The Mantra

Visibility.
Visibility.
Visibility.

That's the mantra lawyers should repeat to themselves first thing before they climb down from their beds in the morning to go about their daily business. In order to secure a space in people's heads, you have to be visible to them. In order to be visible to them, you have to be *"out there"*. They have to identify and associate your face and name with something. Little wonder many celebrities do the best they can to remain in the limelight, even if it means going on self-destructive gimmicks to prove their space in the minds and hearts of people.

Imagine a person unlocking his phone first thing in the morning and he's reading from you via his Facebook feed. You ran a Facebook live event to explain the newest development in the Law that was just passed by the Senate. The same person watches this video, then forgets about it and moves on with his work for the day. Later, he comes across an e-flyer for a conference; your face appears on the flyer as one of the expert panelists, and you're a discussant on some issue. This person nods and then forgets about you. Later the same week, he conducts an online search about how to register a company in so-so city and your comprehensive company registration guide of 5 thousand words crops up to educate him on everything he needs to know. Luckily, the information is on your law firm website; he clicks through some pages and notes that you are into corporate-commercial legal practice.

From these constant run-ins with your brand messaging through an omni-channel approach, he's gotten to "know" you. If and when a legal issue comes up, you are the first person he's going to think of immediately. With this hypothetical individual, you have closed him as a qualified prospect even before he reaches out for your services.

So, answer this question: as an attorney, why won't you learn to market yourself and your law practise to the world?

For those few attorneys that understand legal marketing and devise the best legal strategies to market themselves to the wider world out there, they reap the benefits more than attorneys who merely sit back and rely on their status as professionals for their career growth.

Managing the Fee Earners

Review your Staff over the Years.

Question

How many of your law firm's associates leave every year? Do you lose more associates to your competitors more than you think is normal or more than you like? If the answer is yes, then whatever you and your law firm is doing is not working. If it were working, then the associates in the law firm would not be leaving and setting up camp with competitors or even smaller firms that cannot hold a candle to your firm's practise.

What is your recruiting and retention strategy? Do you even have one? Obviously this cannot be handled in this book because each law firm is different; jurisdictions differ and there are several other factors to consider.

COMPENSATION OF ATTORNEYS

1. Are our attorney fees competitive? _____ yes _____ no.

2. If yes, how can you tell that the fees you pay your attorneys are competitive? Have you conducted surveys or research to discover if other firms within your range pay better? _____ yes _____ no.

3. How can you make your attorney pay competitive to fall in line with what the competitors do or even better?
_____

4. Do your attorneys complain of fees? _____ yes _____ no.

5. Do we offer profit sharing? _____ yes _____ no.

6. Do we offer end-year bonuses or what we call the 13th month pay? _____ yes _____ no.

7. Do we compensate our attorneys for bringing in new work? _____ yes _____ no.

8. Do we pay our attorneys for the work they put in as overtime work or when they work during the weekends? _____ yes _____ no.

9. Do we understand and appreciate the financial obligations of our attorneys and ensure that we try to make them as comfortable as possible? _____ yes _____ no.

Your answers to the above questions can give you an idea in the direction your law firm is headed and whether you should continue with the path you're going, or whether there is need for you to change your operating methods.

These questions are merely a guide; a more in-depth scrutiny into your specific situation would yield answers that can help set you on the right track.

FIRM CULTURE

It's the unspoken term that a lot of attorneys have in their minds but say nothing about, or they whisper about it in online chat rooms and forums. They also pen down their thoughts on "firm culture" on anonymous review Employee sites like Glassdoor and Indeed.

Firm culture of a law firm: how does the law firm operate? What are the hours? Is there a work-life balance? Are the hours unreasonable? Is there micromanagement? Must it be thus: "This was the way I was treated during my pupillage years and so I have to reciprocate the gesture to my employees"? Are the partners open to ideas from the junior associates or are they completely closed off? Are the lead attorneys and partners abusive to the lawyers who work in their law firms? Do the lawyers form a core part of decision making in these law firms?

Firm culture isn't often talked about in the media for professional services firms except for the exceptionally bad cases where a law firm's culture was so horrendous, the dirty linen was hung to dry in the public. And when these happen, it is taken as an extremely embarrassing moment for the legal profession. Everyone comes out to share their opinion on the "inappropriateness" of the behaviour. It is something that is usually swept under the rug because it is a sensitive issue people do not like talking about for any reason, so it becomes a Bar embarrassment if and when the issue arises in public.

So, asides the pay perks and other benefits of working with a law firm, there is another extremely integral point that attorneys should consider very important: the culture. What is it like, working there? What are the shared experiences of the lawyers that work in these firms?

A culture of internal bickering, back-biting, politics, and abuse to staff, is unwelcome and makes for a horrible work environment most attorneys would want to walk away from if and when the chance presents itself. A thriving atmosphere of learning, camaraderie and good work ethics where everyone is understood and works according to their strengths, is a culture worth sustaining. In this latter case, attorneys usually leave these firms if a much better opportunity calls, or if they are ready to take on a different career path from what they're doing already. Or, perhaps they are ready to go and set up their own legal consultancy practise.

For firms with high turnover of employees, there is always something usually lurking underneath the surface. Many former employees may usually be reluctant to spill the beans, but that doesn't mean that there isn't something lurking beneath the surface in many of these cases. It may be the poor work-life balance in the firm, or it could the case of toxic co-workers, or toxic work culture that have attorneys grappling with stomach ulcers, but it is often something that necessitates an employee walking away from the firm without looking back.

Does your law firm have a culture? If yes, what is it like? If your answer is no, then note that no culture is actually a culture on its own. It's just unconsciously defined though inadvertently. If the answer is still no, study these questions and come up with answers: what is working in your law firm like for your law firm associates? I mean—really? Not the front that is presented to members of the public, but really and truly what it means to work with your law firm?

The answers may be surprising.

Helping the Client Win

Law has gone beyond the practise of merely going to courts to douse the legal fires of clients. It has gone beyond mere preparation of countless hundreds of pages of documentation by solicitors or working in a purely legal capacity to do the work of the legal clients of the law firm.

The upward mobility of clients, the increasing sophistication of these legal services consumers, all point to the need for a one-stop shop for professional services for these clients, from advisory to compliance and other service disciplines.

Little wonder a lot of lawyers have argued that law should be inter-disciplinary; that lawyers should take a multi or inter-disciplinary approach in the study of Law when searching for areas of specialization: Law & Finance; Law & Information Technology; Law & Business Consulting; Law & Marketing; Law & Digital Strategy. The point is that it could be the practise of law intermixed with another discipline that may be seemingly unrelated, thus giving you seemingly disparate skill sets but which makes sense in the future or in the long run, depending on the way one wants to look at it.

A great many number of lawyers have taken the conventional approach that law should remain on a grand pedestal; that it should remain unsullied by the studies of other disciplines. A greater number of people take the view that today's world have need for a more diverse slew of skills they can arm themselves with. It is not about having certificates or qualifications; it is now about marrying seemingly disparate skills with others or different disciplines. In the short run, you will probably think that it makes no meaning for a lawyer to have deep industry knowledge of the startup world, but in the long run, it could make a lot of sense because start-ups would ordinarily prefer to retain the services of counsel that deeply understands their industry, rather than a lawyer that does not.

The Future of Work

Lawyers have always prided themselves on the fact that they stay behind their chairs in their corner offices or homes, handling the work of their clients. However, in the current 4th Internet Revolution, that view or ideal has been toppled and will forever remain unseated from its pedestal. With alternative legal services providers, and even productized legal services packages across the world, lawyers have learned—or at least deemed it fit to note—that things are different. In order to compete, lawyers have to become more grounded in the World generally, than in the restrictive spectre of their law practise. There are changes to the workforce, and this is reflecting even in the legal services industry.

Blockchain, Artificial Intelligence, Machine Learning, Information Technology, FinTech, Strategy, data analysis and a whole slew of other seemingly disparate skill sets and knowledge areas are making their way into Law, with many more lawyers delving into these relatively new areas and disparate disciplines that seemingly have "nothing" to do with the legal profession.

How Does Multiple Skills help a Lawyer?

A lawyer that has no knowledge of the business world has no business engaging in advisory for a business entity. A lawyer that does not understand the upstream and downstream sectors of the petroleum industry, alongside the various aspects of oil prospecting, licensing and exploration, has no business advising an oil company on its upstream or downstream work. A lawyer that does not understand Information Technology and the multi-faceted parts of it, has no business advising a Big Data Analytics firm on cybersecurity laws and compliance issues.

From the above, it is pertinent to see that each industry has specific guidelines and sets of rules that govern them. In order for the lawyer to be able to help the client win in their chosen industrial exploits or service sectors, it is pertinent that the lawyer breaths and lives that industry or sector.

So, the multiple skills that can help a lawyer are skills that relate to the work they do in different sectors and industries.

Questions

If a consulting company has legal issues that accrue in the course of their work—whether on-site or off-site—for their clients, who would become involved in that client brief? An outside counsel that does not understand the workings of the client's business structure or someone who does?

Please note that in many cases, consulting companies have a marked reputation for gobbling the best and brightest legal minds (read: Lawyers) to work within their various consulting practise areas: practise consulting, management consulting, risk analysis & management, business analysis, or even in their extensive Knowledge Base departments.

BCG, McKinsey & Company, KPMG, PwC, Deloitte, alongside the other larger consulting firms across the globe have slews of bright young lawyers working for them on the various aspects of their consulting practise. As these young lawyers work within these companies on the areas they deem worthy and interested enough to handle briefings and make a difference in the lives on the companies' clients on, these lawyers keep sharpening both their legal skill sets and other skills so they can perform optimally and over-achieve on the client engagements they handle.

So, back to the question: if a consulting company has legal issues that arise out of a client engagement for a client, who do they call? They probably already have brilliant, constantly learning lawyers working within their teams who can dissect the finer points of these engagements and tackle the legal issues that arise from them . . . with sharp teeth. Outside counsel may (and ordinarily *will*) be able to handle the legal aspect of the work, but their own in-house legal gurus who have mastered their clients' industries will do the job better. This is simply so because these latter set have a deeper industry grasp of their clients' sector operations, they understand the nuances of those specific sectors and they understand how to manoeuvre their way around business issues that crop up within those sectors. That makes them more suited for work within that sector.

The Overriding Factor

Companies are in business to win. They are in business to make maximum returns on their investments in the different ventures they operate. Businesses are always looking for ways to get deeper slices of their target market, and many even devise and implement global expansion strategies that get them working in other Jurisdictions. What this means is that businesses are in business to win; they are there to make more money and influence their target community into loving and using their products/services.

With the above consideration in place, a lawyer would do well to note that companies want people on their team that will help them win. If a group of persons approach you as an attorney to incorporate a company for them, the smaller slice of the work would be to merely incorporate the company, prepare and file all statutory forms to accompany the registration, and the work is done.

If however, you have a deep industry grasp of their chosen industry, understands their operating market, and knows strategies that will be good for the client, it is imperative to bring them out. Deep thinking and proffering of solutions will mark you out as an "insider", someone that understands the business the same way the company executive does, and that earns you a place at the table in the long run. It opens the avenue for long-term work as the company scales and deepens its operations. You become indispensable. Once indispensable, the relationship is cemented because that company would be hard pressed to cut off its working arms before thinking of cutting you off.

Ditching the Entitlement Mentality: No One Owes you Anything

You have to take the time to understand this concept: no one owes you anything. Many lawyers think that because of their professional qualifications, they are going to get clients without having to do anything to further their practice and get known to the world out there.

Perhaps clients may come and break down your doors in a perfect world, just perhaps. But note that in a perfect world there may never be the need for a lawyer in the first place. Or, more specifically, specific brands of lawyers.

So, a lawyer out there becomes like any other professional who the world owes nothing to. They have to make their own way. They have to get into the red ocean and fight the sharks for their slice of the sherry or they will be gobbled up.

The Problem

Many people in different jurisdictions lack a "legal culture" or "legal awareness". They do not see the legal professional as someone that is integral to their business efforts such that they always need the services/advice of a legal practitioner for their varied needs. In such a situation it becomes more difficult for the lawyer to convince the potential client of the worth of his services; in cases such as these the person only takes an active interest in legal representation if he has a particularly specific and insurmountable legal problem that needs to be handled. That is the time the lawyer comes in as emergency problem solver to get rid of the problem the same way a surgeon would work to quickly get rid of a ruptured appendix.

That makes the legal practitioner discouraged at some point. He has to sell harder, and only to sell at specific times, particularly when the potential client's needs is most urgent and needs immediate attention.

It should be noted that this section was headed "The Problem". That is so because the scenario painted within it presents a unique problem that lawyers across various jurisdictions grapple with. People simply may not and do not want to buy legal services unless they absolutely have to, for specific scenarios. But still, if and when potential clients need to be sold to at this particular point in the sales funnel, it is easier to sell to them then—at that high point when they actively and urgently require legal representation for a matter—than it would be to ordinarily sell to them when they feel they have no need for the services of a lawyer. The reason is because they then have no choice other than to search around for legal representation, and if a particular firm or attorney comes up on their radar, they are likely to make the requisite contact.

There are no guarantees that this prospect will buy, but at least the offerings are there for him to make an informed decision. This can work in the lawyer's favour or not.

The Marketing Aversion

Lawyers are known for their marked aversion to marketing and other promotional activities that relate to projecting their professional and technical expertise out there to potential individual and institutional clients. Lawyers who subscribe to this school of thought believe that it is beneath them to engage in promotional activities for their professional services. They further compound it with the belief that professional qualifications, technical capabilities and stellar work delivery to clients, should be enough indicators that they are highly skilled at what they do and should be retained for more work or be referred for future work.

In the past, the above approach may work because the legal services industry was not so competitive that lawyers had to absolutely sell hard. Today, the legal services industry has become competitive, so competitive that lawyers and law firms are grappling with each other for market share. Alternative legal services providers and DYI systems that are now in place compound the problem, because many people has seen the need to eliminate the use of lawyers altogether because there are alternative routes they can go for the services they need.

In the light of the above harrowing circumstances, professional services firms have learned how to sell, and lawyers have joined the fray. Now, lawyers who "sell" better than their counterparts are revered; they are well known, they have connections and contacts that open out to become prospective clients and referral sources.

The larger percentage of lawyers who are inherently averse to marketing get to see the fewer, supposedly "elite" lawyers in their Bar Associations making headlines, attending conferences, keynoting conferences and seminars, appearing on TV to talk about Sector occurrences while proffering industry insights into these situations, making headway in Trade publications, receiving awards, and being in general: "awesome". In most cases the larger crop of lawyers are disgruntled by this development and, in many cases, go out of their way to grumble, as if these supposedly "elite" lawyers are taking hefty slices of the legal market and leaving them with crumbs of the legal services market. These "crumbs" are the less revered halls of courtroom litigation.

In many cases, the complaining lawyers are often right. Companies, multinational conglomerates and high net worth individuals tend to go for these "elite", visible lawyers, while the others remain in the shadows. This boils down to a prevailing thought: as a lawyer, no one owes you anything. The mere fact that a lawyer is a working professional does not mean that clients should fall over themselves in order to brief the lawyers.

Quote to Note:

"People who are well known are magnets that draw others in".

Remember previous paragraphs, or at least the part where it was reiterated that no one owes a lawyer anything. It is the lawyer's duty to ditch that mentality, understand that the legal market—like every other services and products market—favour those who seem to have their fingers in different slices of various pies, and start making moves to stand out.

Quote to Note:

"*A big fish or a colourful fish is easier to stand out in a pond than the ones that blend in*".

Ditching that entitlement mentality and working to build brand reputation and visibility will aid any marketing-minded lawyer in their race to the top of the food chain.

It is because no one owes you anything that you have to fight hard to gain top-of-mind awareness in the minds of people and remain there. It is because no one owes you anything in the course of your professional work as a lawyer that you have to ensure that you get to make them know you and the work you do.

Conclusion

The legal profession is one of the "esteemed" professional paths a wanna-be professional would like to be involved in. In the past, it had prestige, so much so that people regarded Law as the path to professional heaven. Now, the reality is different. The horizon is bleaker. The waters are redder and the currents seemingly less friendly than they used to be. Artificial Intelligence, alternative legal providers, DYI websites, large number of lawyers and the descent of professional services into competition and aggressive marketing has changed the equation.

In order to reach to the highest peak within a relatively shorter period of time, lawyers have to learn to "compete" and "market"; two terms that was previously anathema to lawyers. They have to learn to put themselves in the spotlight. They have to learn to thrive in their law firms' "Media Rooms", as law firms are becoming full publishing houses of legal information for the legal services marketplace. They have to learn the rules of marketing, advertising and competition and adapt localized strategies that can help them yield positive results for their efforts and marketing spend.

The tides have changed. The wind of change has blown across the legal services horizon. Times have turned the legal profession into a cutthroat market where the ones with the sharpest teeth and more muscular arms win. And those law firms with sharp teeth—the ones with streamlined marketing tactics and strong marketing perceptions—have their tools and strategies with which they can win and get large cuts of market share. Others sit back in their chairs in their offices and grumble about those make studious effort to gain market share while waiting for "clients" to come with their legal issues.

For lawyers, those that learn to market themselves and have mastered the subtle art of "selling without selling" are the ones that get to sit on boards, get free invites to speak on conferences, get invited to share their opinions on TV and radio stations. They are the ones that everyone talks about and everyone wants to be like without necessarily knowing how to make that happen.

You may be conservative as a lawyer and you are comfortable with that. If that is the case, then sure thing: there is no problem. Keep being you and keep on doing your thing. If however, you feel boxed into the box of the profession and you would like to spring out, shine bright, and get noticed as the wild flower in a large field of plain white daisies, then take the time to deeply digest this book.

About the Author

Kingsley Ugochukwu Ani is a lawyer, writer and business development consultant with experience working with C-Suite executives to devise and implement marketing strategies for business operations. He's spent his entire professional life directing and developing strategy and market development programs for busy attorneys and professionals. He believes in the unconstrained power of the Internet which can be leveraged for professional and Firm success in a congested world where everyone is trying to outbid themselves. To find out more about his consulting services, call him on +2347035074930 or email him on anikingsley@kabbiz.com

www.ingramcontent.com/pod-product-compliance
Lightning Source LLC
Chambersburg PA
CBHW030640220526
45463CB00004B/1586